Model Railroading Handbook

Volume II

Model Railroading Handbook

Volume II

Robert Schleicher

Chilton Book Company   Radnor, Pennsylvania

Published in Radnor, Pa., by Chilton Book Company and
simultaneously in Don Mills, Ontario, Canada,
by Thomas Nelson & Sons, Ltd.

Manufactured in the United States of America

Library of Congress Cataloging in Publication Data

Schleicher, Robert H.
    Model railroading handbook.
    Includes indexes.
    1. Railroads—Models.   I. Title.
TF197.S34   1975   625.1'9   75-12688
ISBN 0-8019-6167-X (v. I, hardcover)
ISBN 0-8019-6168-8 (v. I, paperback)
ISBN 0-8019-6717-1 (v. II, hardcover)
ISBN 0-8019-6718-X (v. II, paperback)

1 2 3 4 5 6 7 8 9 0   7 6 5 4 3 2 1 0 9 8

Contents

Layouts, Locomotives and Rolling Stock

Model railroading, to me, is more of an art form than the best oil or watercolor work on canvas or paper. If I did paint, my subjects would be old buildings, mountains' majesty and steam-powered railroads in action. I can achieve better results with miniatures than I can with a paintbrush, and the finished art has three dimensions rather than just two. There really is another side to that mountain if I choose to model it, and those trains don't just *look* as if they can move, they *do* move and just as impressively as the real ones did in 1910 or 1930 or 1970. I don't consider myself a model maker or model engineer or model technology fan; I create three-dimensional animated works of art. I may very well be the only one who thinks my work is good enough to be classified as art, but I'm the only one I want to please, so the rest of the world can keep its opinion of my model railroad.

You may prefer the actual construction of models above all else, or you may prefer to work out miniature engineering marvels or create a computerized model railroad. If you do, you and I share the same hobby even if we don't envision the final goals as the same. In fact, my model railroad is far more of a vision than a reality right now. In most respects I'm more of an armchair model railroader than most, but that doesn't change my image of the hobby that occupies most of my leisure time. I have learned to my satisfaction that this is a hobby for just about anyone who wants to create something with his or her hands. There are about a half-million of us serious hobbyists, and we spend nearly $200 million a year in our quiet way. So welcome to the hobby of model railroading.

MORE MODEL RAILROADING

This is the second volume in the *Model Railroading Handbook* series, and you have every right to wonder why one book isn't enough. If you have some experience in the hobby, you know there are dozens of other publications that deal with model railroading, and that none of them attempts to cover the whole spectrum the way this one does.

Arts, Crafts and Engineering

Model railroading is a simple enough hobby to be covered by the four-page pamphlets that are included in some train sets, but there are enough facets of it to literally fill a bookshelf with little duplication of information.

You could learn all the basics about building a complete model railroad from Volume I of this series. This volume carries on from there to present additional techniques for slightly more refined layout planning, operation, rolling stock and locomotive construction, structure and scenery construction, and wiring that have made the hobby more enjoyable for others. I've also tried to illustrate some of the ideas that could only be mentioned in Volume I and to introduce some new concepts like dioramas and simplified signaling systems. My goal has been to discover as many methods as I could of making the hobby simpler. If you want to complicate it with scratch-built locomotives or computerized electronics or board-by-board buildings, then do so and enjoy your own fulfillment of the promise of pleasure model railroading offers.

Fig. 1-1 The freight car classification yard is one of the fascinating symbols of real railroading that inspires modelers to build a duplicate in miniature. The remnants of the roof walk removal program date this scene in Minneapolis to the early 1970s.

There are times, in this hobby, when the goals of simple enjoyment and real railroading in miniature are hard to balance. Operating track-side signals and a layout for lots of miniature mileage are two examples of that dilemma you'll find in later chapters. You'll see as simple a signal system as I could find in Chapter IX, and an HO scale empire in Chapter XIII that packs almost four scale miles of trackage into an area equal to a 1½-car garage. You can simplify the signal system still further by using only dummy signals with steady green or red lights, and the double-track portion of the Ma & Pa track plan can go. You'll give up the fascination of seeing the signals' recognition of a train's passing and miss the thrill of main-line

operation with these simplifications, but you'll still be a model railroader. You'll find many more choices in two books than you would in one, even more in a bookshelf of books. My purpose in presenting the material I do is to give you what I feel are the best possible choices for a "best" signal system or a "best" HO scale model railroad plan. You'll have to decide whether to agree (by building what I suggest) or disagree by building something to suit your own tastes, or to ignore the choosing completely by remaining just an armchair model railroader. The hobby of model railroading has enough scope to fulfill any of those choices with pleasure.

You'll see some very fine modeling on these pages. You'll also see the results of clever use of space, kits and materials, and that's one of the most important lessons you can learn. I know far too many model railroaders who spend so much time working on the benchwork or track for a large layout that they don't have time for the fun the hobby has to offer. Remind yourself, if you must, to allot enough time in your modeling schedule to sit back and admire what you have accomplished. Why bother to spend all that time making your models look realistic and then not bother to even look at them, let alone at their realism? If you're interested enough in model railroading to have even read this far, you are fortunate enough to be one of the very few who have not lost that childlike innocence of imagination. Models exist because humans enjoy the feelings that come from imagining that the models are real. Take your pick of being a giant or imagining you are small enough to sit inside that locomotive. There's a thrill in either thought, and that thrill is even greater when you know you've created the scene you are viewing.

Model railroading is unusual among hobbies and pastimes, in that you can derive as much satisfaction from looking at what you make as you can from making it. Some model railroaders even enjoy operating their railroads *more* than they do building them, and there are enough ready-to-run and easy-to-build models available to make them as happy as the modeler who just finished carving a Big Boy articulated from strips and bars of raw brass. I do hope you'll learn some techniques and shortcuts that will make modeling easier, but more than that, I hope you'll learn how much fun there is in model railroading.

ONE STEP BEYOND

When you have assembled enough kits to feel you are capable of adding something that's not in the box, then you're ready to become a real model railroader. That first personal touch should be some weathering on your cars, locomotives and buildings as outlined in Chapter III. Remember that those same techniques can be used to weather snap-together track sections. The weathering techniques, more than any other single skill, can make even ready-made plastic models look almost as good as completely scratch-built miniatures. Weathering is that one step which will carry your models beyond the realm of toys to make them true museum-quality miniatures. Somehow your mind can ignore a lot of missing detail, perhaps even skip the giant third rail and strange proportions of Lionel O scale equipment, when the coloring of the real thing is there in the form of realistic "dust" and "dirt." You can weather models effectively with spray cans and paintbrushes using techniques shown in Volume I, but the process is far more effective and easier if you buy an airbrush. Your first nonmodel item of investment (after the basic knife/tweezers, pliers/screwdriver/glue purchase) should, then, be an airbrush like those in Chapter III.

When you've mastered the art of making a stock kit or ready-built model look realistic, you may want to go on to create your own unique models utilizing the cross-kit or conversion techniques in Chapters II, III and XIV. The weathering technique will give you a chance to be truly creative in a two-dimensional sense; cross-kits allow you to have some creative expression in three dimensions, using ready-built parts to make something that's not available anywhere as a kit or a ready-built. Here you'll begin to learn the precision that is the earmark of a true model builder as you make cuts and joints that are *your* choices, not some model manufacturer's. Frankly, it's best to try cross-kitting on a structure kit first, because the choice of where to cut isn't as critical as it with a locomotive or a piece of rolling stock. If you make a mistake on a structure, you can always add a patch of simulated wood siding, a brick surface or even tarpaper—cutting mistakes happen on full-size structures too, and those are the ways that some of them are corrected. You will need some of the precision measuring instruments of this hobby, however, even for the cross-kit structures. Proper tools, including the ones that allow you to measure fits and clearances precisely, are the next investment you should make in nonmodel items (Fig. 1-2).

Steel scale rulers graduated in feet and inches are available for all the popular scales. Walthers has a 12-inch-long ruler for N, TT, S, HO and O scales. General has a foot-long one with HO, S and O scale markings, and Flint has a 6-inch one with N scale markings and other N scale data. For measurements where you need to be accurate within a scale inch or a fraction of a scale inch, you'll need a micrometer (useful in any scale), PFM's vernier calipers with HO or O scale calibrations or Walthers's clear plastic Micro Measure. If you have a conventional pair of vernier calipers, you can use them, but if you're going to make

an investment, then buy the PFM vernier calipers for HO or O scale. The cheap way out is to just purchase a scale ruler, Walthers's Micro Measure and a magnifying glass to read them.

While I'm on the subject of measuring devices, it's a good time to mention the NMRA standards gauge and Kadee's coupler height gauge. These last two are really tools to help eliminate derailments, but you'll also want to use them when you're completing any car or locomotive. The standards gauge will tell you HO modelers whether the wheels or drivers are in correct gauge and help to judge coupler height. The Kadee coupler height gauge, like the NMRA gauge, can also be used to mea-

Fig. 1-2 Precision tools are needed for both accurately scaled models and for derailment-free operation. General's HO, S and O scale ruler, Flint's N scale ruler, Walthers's Micro-Measure card, a micrometer, PFM's HO scale vernier calipers, the NMRA HO scale standards gauge and Kadee's HO scale coupler height jigs (on a length of HO track) are shown here.

sure track rail spacing but there are better gauges than either one for track laying. Use the NMRA gauge for checking switches, for wheel sets and tunnel clearances and the Kadee gauge for checking coupler heights.

MINIATURE MODEL RAILROADS

When you make a model railroad that's only a foot square, that's a miniature. I'm not talking about absurd layouts around a hat brim but what are called dioramas, complete scenes or vignettes that are essentially a miniature model railroad. Most dioramas include about 2 to 6 inches of the "ground" that surrounds a structure, enough to incorporate the track and the road next to the building and a suggestion of more terrain yet to come. There's no reason, however, why a diorama cannot include just a length or two of track with some typical line-side scenery like a drainage ditch, old ties, fencing and weeds, or even better, some just-burned weeds.

I have heard and read that dioramas are constructed mainly to add some "scenery" around a structure to make photos seem more realistic. You'll find dioramas in the color photo pages and in Chapter VI that have been used for photography. I was the photographer, and frankly, a diorama makes a poor place to take a picture of a model. Even a 2 x 4-foot modular model railroad is better. Your eye may stop at the edge of the diorama, but your imagination takes over from there; a camera lens doesn't have that kind of imagination. A diorama is certainly the best place to display a structure and a car or locomotive or a few of them. It's a good way to learn all the techniques of the hobby including scenery on a small scale, and your time will not be wasted because the scene can be fitted neatly into any larger model railroad you may build later.

The diorama can put an end to the excuse that "I just don't have room for a model railroad." Everyone has at least a dresser top with room for one diorama, and you may even want to build or buy a bookcase to display a dozen or more such scenes. There is no

better way to build a structure than on a piece of ½-inch Homosote, where you can include the building's foundation and be sure that there's none of that toylike look of a structure sitting on (rather than in) the "ground." When it comes time to add that structure to your basement-sized layout, just cut a hole in the layout's roadbed large enough to fit the diorama and later blend the surrounding scenery to match that on the diorama.

One of the nicest plusses about dioramas is that they can move with you regardless of where you go, so you can retain at least those portions of any layout you may build anywhere. You may rearrange your structure dioramas on that next layout so that the most time-consuming portion of layout construction, building buildings, need only be done once—all assuming, of course, that you were wise enough to attach the diorama to the layout with a few screws rather than glue.

There's yet another way to go model railroading in the space of a bookshelf rather than a basement—modules. The NTRAK concept of 2 x 4-foot and 2 x 6-foot interchangeable portions of a model railroad has taken hold, for N scale at least, and there are now over 200 modules around the world that can be joined to each other any time two or more NTRAK enthusiasts get together. There are usually about a dozen regional gatherings of NTRAK modules where there may be 10 to 50 modules joined into layouts ranging from 4 x 20 feet to 54 x 96 feet! The basic NTRAK standard stipulates three main-line tracks across the front edge of a 2 x 4, 2 x 6 or 2 x 8-foot module; the trackage and scenery on the rest of the module can be anything the builder would like.

The same idea has been applied to HO, HOn3, S, O and On3 modular layouts by clubs all across the country. You'll find some of the established groups listed in Chapter VI. You can build your own 2 x 4-foot module to any of these groups' standards and connect your railroad to theirs (or for that matter to other modules of your own) to complete a club-size layout. Some of these clubs have permanent halls or other rented areas, where they can leave at least a portion of their mem-

Fig. 1-3   The "cookie cutter" method of benchwork combines the use of a flat plywood tabletop with open grid construction for uphill and downhill grades. The plywood roadbed subbase should be cut with a saber saw or jigsaw before the roadbed or the track is in place.

bers' modules assembled into an operating layout. Most of the modular groups simply rent space several times during the year so the members can assemble their modules for a day or two of operation. These get-togethers are often planned for the various regional and national conventions of the National Model Railroad Association. You could build five or six 2 x 4-foot modules, in any scale, and a rack or bookcase to house them in just 2 x 4 feet of floor space. When you want to operate, just get together with some other owners of modules, or gather only your own in an empty garage or basement. Again, it's a way of insuring a lifetime model railroad regardless of where you might move.

DO IT RIGHT THE FIRST TIME

When you finally do find the place and the space for that first permanent model railroad, you'll be wise if you take advantage of the mistakes of others. Building your buildings on removable dioramas is one way to avoid those mistakes; opting for a modular type of layout where you can literally build your whole layout (in modules) to a plan is another sure-fire way to a layout that works. The diorama idea will work for anyone, but there are those who just don't want the design restrictions that the modules must have. Most of the design methods in this book and in Volume I utilize materials like Homosote and Hydrocal and ground foam that have proven to be the best for countless modelers. There are other concepts, like the walk-around control in Chapter VIII, the walk-in layout designs in Chapter XII and the stall-free switch wiring in Chapter IX that I would recommend that you adopt for any model railroad in any scale to avoid patience-consuming problems. I would include open-grid benchwork and shoulder-level trackwork in that list as well.

There is a strong temptation to simply slap a tabletop on some 1" x 4" supports or to simply use a Ping-Pong table for that first off-the-floor model railroad. This type of flat-top benchwork might save one weekend in building time, but it will give you years of problems. Preplan your railroad utilizing the concepts in Chapter XII, and take that extra week-end to build a framework of 1" x 3' boards on edge to support the subbase for your trackwork. Space the 1 x 3s into squares or rectangles with 18 to 24-inch sides and use number 8 x 1½-inch wood screws rather than nails so you can move some of the 1 x 3s later on. The plywood tabletop or roadbed subbase should be supported about 3 to 6 inches above the 1" x 3" framework to leave room for valleys as well as hills and to give those streams, lakes and rivers someplace to go. Attach 1" x 3" or 1" x 4" risers about every 18 inches or so to elevate the roadbed subbase above the 1 x 3 framework. You can use the "cookie cutter" type of construction to cut the tabletop for grade elevations up from that zero elevation 3 to 6 inches above the framework. Some modelers really do start with a 5 x 9-foot solid tabletop and plan their layout by temporarily laying the track on the tabletop and marking

Fig. 1-4 One-half-inch thick Homosote wallboard is the best roadbed to go beneath any type of track in any scale. Be sure to sand the joints between pieces of Homosote. The legs and main benchwork supports for the Highland Park club's benchwork are 2-inch square steel tubes welded together.

its locations. They then remove the track and use a saber or jigsaw to cut through the plywood to remove it from all the areas except the actual trackwork and the flat building sites. If you've preplanned your layout, you can save a lot of plywood by cutting enough curved and straight sections to match your actual track plan rather than starting with a "full" tabletop.

Most model railroaders prefer to operate their layouts from a standing position so they can walk along with the trains. You won't likely be operating for more than three or four hours at a time, so unless you have some physical handicap, it's best to plan the layout height for stand-up viewing and operation. It's also a lot easier to work on the track and scenery when you don't have to bend over to reach a layout the height of a Ping-Pong table. The actual elevation of the benchwork will depend on the highest track on the layout. In the case of the Ma & Pa plan in Chapter XIII, the highest track is 19 inches at the York yard, and most of the low track is about 4 inches above zero. I would suggest placing the York yard exactly at your own shoulder level, since it's your layout. If you are unusually tall, then provide a few stools or small platforms so shorter folk can see your entire layout. If your layout has less of a difference in elevation, you might want to establish the maximum height about 4 to 6 inches below your shoulder level—the rather large difference in elevations on that Ma & Pa layout dictates a fairly high level for York so that the rest of the layout won't be too low. You will also discover that your models look much more realistic when viewed from a level somewhere near that of a scale model person—we seldom see real trains from the top of a mountain, and when we do, they tend to look like models!

The actual open-grid benchwork can be built in sections small enough to fit through the door of the layout room and bolted or screwed into a single room-filling table. Don't make the sections much larger than 2½ x 6 feet, regardless, or they'll be too heavy to carry after all the roadbed and plaster scenery is installed. Some of those subtables can be different heights above the floor on a layout

like the Ma & Pa; the open-grid benchwork's upper edge at York only needs to be about 4 inches below the York rail heights to provide support for the hidden Dallastown trackwork. The benchwork below Delta, however, should be at least 14 inches below the Delta rail tops to be low enough for the hidden trackwork below Delta. In other words, the plywood subbase at Delta will have to be supported above the open-grid benchwork by 1" x 3" or 1" x 4" risers about 13 inches high, plus the length needed to attach them to the open-grid benchwork itself. The risers to support York would have to be even higher if the open-grid benchwork in that area were not raised above the floor about 9 inches more than the benchwork for the rest of the layout. The Ma & Pa is definitely a layout for experienced modelers—you won't find the layouts in Chapter XII nearly so complex, although most of them do demand some change in track elevation above a zero elevation. The important point here is that you keep the trackwork as near your eye level as you can and that you build it in an open-grid framework to allow room for rivers and valleys below track level.

PERIOD MODELING

Model railroading is above all a pastime that is supposed to provide enjoyment to the participants. In a word, model railroading is fun—at least it's supposed to be. I'm about to suggest some rules that you should at least consider for the hobby, whether you simply buy ready-built plastic locomotives, cars, structures and scenery, or if you scratch-build everything from sticks and bits of metal or plastic. Model railroading is one of those "mature" hobbies that has been around long enough to have plenty of products to satisfy anyone's interest in any kind of train. You can, for example, buy ready-to-run HO scale versions of locomotives ranging from the two little 4-4-0s that touched pilots at Promintory, Utah, in 1869 to the latest Amtrak electric, with open-platform coaches and Amtrak Am-coaches to match. You can also operate those

Fig. 1-5   If you are clever enough to plan your layout before building it, the open-grid type of construction is the most economical and the best base for later scenery.

two passenger trains side-by-side on your layout, but they're both going to look a little silly because it's not a sight you would expect to see in real life. The time you spend building and detailing your models will to a large extent be wasted if you insist on operating it in a toylike manner. The realism vanishes when you try to mix too much into one model railroad. Nobody has enough imagination to span the century of trains between those examples of early 4-4-0s and modern Amtrak trains. At best, your model railroad will look like an operating train museum rather than a real railroad in miniature.

If you expect to create a realistic model railroad, then you are going to have to select a definite time period for that railroad and its equipment. You'll have a lot more latitude with the structures as long as you stay away from the very modern or the very old. Buildings of the 1880 to 1940 period were often

built to the same architectural styles. If you cannot decide on a certain favorite time period, or if you just don't want to, then at least try to keep the buildings in that simple brick, stone and frame timeless style. The locomotives and rolling stock that operate on the real railroads have undergone some rather sweeping changes over the last hundred years, and none quite so great as in the last decade. Model railroading grew from a 100,000-member hobby into today's size, which is triple that, during a period when the railroads were undergoing the greatest changes of their history. You could operate all the diesels and steam engines and the rolling stock that was available to modelers in 1956 on your layout and not be too far removed from the mixture that appeared on the real railroads in 1956. Times have changed.

The real railroads of the seventies are almost totally unlike those of the sixties or earlier eras. It's true that many of the diesels and freight cars and even some passenger cars from the fifties are still in operation, but *all* that equipment has been altered so much that a photo of a freight yard of 1970 or later cannot be mistaken for a photo of an earlier era. All the real railroads, even a short line like the Maryland & Pennsylvania, have updated their heralds (in modern terms, their logos) and repainted their cars and locomotives in schemes that didn't exist a decade or so ago. Some of those modern images replaced heralds and paint schemes that had been in use since the 1800s. Entire railroads have disappeared, with one giant replacing as many as a dozen older lines. Even if you do find a boxcar that's painted boxcar red with, perhaps, a Baltimore & Ohio herald, you'll find that its ladders have been cut off halfway up the sides and that the roof walk—the single most visible part of a model—has been removed to comply with one of the safety programs of the seventies. If you do find a GP-9 or RS-2 or E-8 diesel from the first generation of diesels in the forties and fifties, it will be painted in one of the modern one-color schemes like the Penn Central's black or Conrail's new blue. You might find a steam locomotive's tender or a wood boxcar painted silver or yellow in some derelict work train, but don't even bother to try to find a wood freight car in its original colors. You wouldn't even have known about Conrail or the Penn Central or the Burlington Northern or 3,000-horsepower diesels like the GP-45 in 1956 or even in 1966.

Before I get specific about the more definitive periods of real railroading, consider one way around the dilemma of loving all kinds of realistic miniature trains but only being able to run about ten years' worth. You can arrange your locomotives and rolling stock into the time periods I'm about to suggest, so that only the correct cars and locomotives ever appear together. If you keep your structures in that architectural limbo I mentioned—one, incidentally, where most of the railroad-related buildings fit—you can bring, say, 1955 on stage for a few operating sessions, then change equipment for a session of, say, 1975

operations. You may also want to replace some of the trucks, automobiles and billboards to keep everything as accurate and authentic for that time period as possible. If you wish, the time period can even be changed gradually; as the steam locomotives disappear into the tunnels never to appear again, the newer diesels can begin to appear. If you have the equipment and the interest, you can even run the gamut from those 1869 engines right through to Amtrak and Conrail. The important point is that you don't try to mix Conrail equipment with still-active steam locomotives and expect the scene to be realistic.

There are also some compromise time periods in which you can operate several overlapping time periods. Examples of most classes of 10-wheelers and consolidations and even Americans survived until the fifties when the almost-modern GP and SD-series diesels had begun to operate. There were still a few heavyweight passenger cars around in 1959 to operate on the local runs while the streamliners traveled the main lines. Set your model railroad's time period in the decade of the fifties, avoid any of the postmerger paint schemes, and you can operate just about any type of equipment. If you prefer all types of steam, including wood burners, to diesels, then settle for the twenties when most of the larger steam locomotive types were introduced but the old-timers still plied the branch lines. If you like all types of diesels including the first-generation SW switchers, FT and E-series hood types and even some of the box cabs from the twenties, then settle on 1965–75 as your decade and combine both merger (except Conrail) and premerger paint schemes of the changeover period. With these general time zones as a background, let's take a look back at some of the milestones of railroad history as they affected the appearance and operation of the real railroads.

LOCOMOTIVE CHRONOLOGY FOR PERIOD MODELING

1850   4-4-0 (American) the most common wheel arrangement with a few 2-4-0s, 4-2-0s, 0-6-0s and 0-8-0s in operation.

1854   Coal becoming a common alternative fuel to wood.

1864   4-6-0 (10-Wheeler) delivered to railroads.

1865   2-6-0 (Mogul) delivered to railroads.

1866   2-8-0 (Consolidation) delivered for heavy freight service.

1897   First 4-4-2 (Atlantic) and 2-8-2 (Mikado) deliveries.

1898   Compound-style locomotives introduced with more power.

1901   First 4-6-2 (Pacific) deliveries.

1902   Oil becoming a common alternative fuel to coal in some areas.

1903   First 2-10-2 (Santa Fe) delivery and first articulateds (a narrow-gauge 0-6-6-0 series of locomotives).

1906   First standard-gauge articulateds (0-6-6-0s and 2-6-6-0s).

1911   First 2-8-8-2 articulated delivered.

1916   First 4-8-2 (Mountain) delivered.

1917   U.S.R.A. Standard locomotive designs introduced.

1924   First 2-10-4 (Texas) delivered.

1925   First Alco/Ingersol Rand 60-ton box cab diesel switchers delivered.

1926   First 4-8-4 (Northern) delivered.

1934   First of the famed Pennsylvania Railroad GG-1 electrics delivered.

1934   First streamliners (the Burlington Zephyr and Union Pacific M10,000) in operation.

1937   Diesel-powered Santa Fe Super Chief and Union Pacific City of San Francisco begin operation. Electro-Motive delivers first NW-1 diesel switchers and E2 A and B unit road engines.

1938   Streamlined (and still steam-powered) Twentieth Century Limited begins operation on New York Central.

1939   Electro-Motive delivers first SW-1 switchers and E3 and FTA and B unit road engines, first Baldwin V01000 switchers.

1940   First Alco RS-1 all-purpose hood diesel delivered.

1942   First 4-8-8-4 (Big Boy) articulated delivered to Union Pacific.

1948   Last Alco steam locomotive built.

1949   First Electro-Motive GP-7 hood all-purpose diesel delivered.

1950   Last Baldwin steam locomotive delivered.

1952   First Electro-Motive six-axle SD-7 hood all-purpose diesel delivered.

1959   Steam operations ended on most U.S. railroads.

1965   Diesel pooling operations and first Electro-Motive SD-45s.

1968   Major mergers begin with formation of Penn Central from New York Central and Pennsylvania Railroads and first unit trains.

1970   Burlington Northern formed from Great Northern; Northern Pacific; Spokane, Portland & Seattle; and Burlington.

1971   Rail Passenger Service Act takes effect to begin Amtrak.

1976   Conrail merges majority of northeastern railroads.

The dates on this chronology are generally those when the locomotive or event first appeared on an American railroad; it usually took another year or more for the change or addition to become noticeable throughout the railroad system. Remember that, in the case of the steam locomotive introduction dates, these were the first engines with that wheel arrangement; some of the 1930-vintage consolidations, for example, were as large as their contemporary Mikados. The overall size of steam locomotives in general grew steadily until 1942. The merger and pooling dates are shown because the resulting effect on the appearance of a typical set of diesels was so profound. Prior to 1964, each railroad kept most of its own diesels on its own tracks; today it is not at all unusual to see Union Pacific diesels in the east and even in Canada. The mergers resulted in a gradual depletion on the variety of colors and heralds on America's locomotives, passenger cars, cabooses and freight cars.

The changes in the locomotives in America were the result of technological advances that affected the railroads' rolling stock as well. All the freight and passenger equipment (except for a few tank cars) was of all-wood construction prior to about 1905. Flat cars, hopper cars, gondolas and tank cars were the first freight equipment to be built from steel, and by the end of World War I, almost all new rolling stock was of all-steel construction. The railroads did revert to wood sides for boxcars, reefers, gondolas and hoppers during World War II, but these cars had external steel bracing and were known as composite designs.

Steel passenger cars appeared in 1907, and those early cars were scribed to simulate wood in the hope of allaying passenger's fears of lightning being attracted to the newfangled equipment. Pullman built its last wood car in 1910, and during that same year the New York Central's Twentieth Century Limited became the first all-steel passenger train. Stainless steel, aluminum and lightweight construction techniques were applied to passenger cars in 1934; most equipment built after 1937 was of the lightweight streamliner design.

Some aspects of technology were slow to take effect on American railroads. Refrigerated cooling has been taken for granted in most American homes for fifty years, but the railroads utilized ice for cooling their refrigerator cars until the sixties. Pacific Fruit Express ordered its first mechanical refrigerator car in 1953 and its last ice-cooled car in 1957. The demise of the ice-cooled car ended the usefulness of the elevated ice platforms from which ice was loaded into the hatches in each corner of the roof of the refrigerator cars. Some of the ice-cooled cars were converted to mechanical

refrigeration, but the reefer car ice hatch was even harder to find than a roof walk by the seventies.

It seems to have taken 20 years or more for the breakthroughs in railroad technology on the chronology chart to take effect. The powerful and efficient U.S.R.A. Mikados of 1917 were the culmination of an 1897 promise. Articulated steam locomotives of 1903 eventually grew into the Big Boys of 1942. The early box cab diesels of the twenties weren't really accepted until the introduction of the FT hood units, which looked almost exactly like F-3 through F-9 diesels of later years, and the SW diesel switchers in 1939. Electric locomotives operated in the late 1800s, but the type didn't reach its peak until the introduction of the GG-1 in 1934. The steam locomotive that operated in the twenties didn't look much like those that extended the usefulness of steam in the late fifties.

To be most effective, a period model railroad should not encompass much more than a decade. If you are interested in what the real railroads did, then do some research on your own, especially on the particular real railroad or railroads that appeal to you the most. There are hundreds of profusely illustrated books on every main-line railroad in North America and others that cover most of the smaller lines. Notice the dates on the photos of scenes you like, and compare those views to whatever locomotives and rolling stock are available, to select the period or periods that you want to include on your model railroad.

THE WOOD BURNER PERIOD

The period from 1850 to about 1880 is one well worth modeling, particularly in HO or O scales, for which there are many kits and ready-built items to make the task easier. The majority of the locomotives would be American (4-4-0) types with a few 10-wheelers and a sample or two of the new consolidations. The pilots would be those long and pointed styles, and the smokestacks would be one or the other of the "balloon" or inverted-funnel shapes like the Congden, cabbage and dia-

Fig. 1-6 A particular period or era can make your entire railroad more credible and therefore more realistic. These 4-4-0s and short freight cars with truss rod underframes and wood sides date this scene in the 1860–1890 era.

mond styles. The cabs and tenders would be painted in bright hues with gold striping. The freight cars would be mostly 28 to 34-footers with even a few surviving four-wheeled cars, and the passenger stock would be in the 45 to 65-foot range and all with open-end platforms. Four of these early freight cars would fit on a siding filled by three of the 40-foot cars of the twenties—a real advantage for the always space-short model railroader. The trains too would be short in keeping with the relatively feeble locomotives. The books *Iron Horses to Promintory* by Gerald M. Best and *Civil War Railroads* by E. P. Alexander have some excellent data on this era. Bachmann, AHM and Mantua offer ready-to-run equipment of this era for HO scale modelers, and MDC has a few passenger car kits.

THE GAY NINETIES

This was the Victorian age and one of the best periods for a model railroad. Any kit or ready-built piece of equipment with a truss rod underframe could be used for a railroad

set in the 1880–1900 period. The locomotives would be slightly less colorful, but to make up for them, blue and silver Russian iron boilers and varnished hardwood cabs with gold lettering were then the current style. Even freight locomotives were still kept in a polished state, and the Janney or MCB couplers of today had finally replaced the link and pin styles of earlier years. Most freight cars were in the 32 to 36-foot range, and passenger cars up to 80 feet were common. Most of the passenger cars still had open platforms, but the narrow enclosed vestibule—Westwood has a few cars like this in HO scale—was standard on the limiteds from about 1893 on.

Ten-wheel high-drivers pulled those limiteds, and 10-wheel low-drivers pulled most of the local passenger trains and even a few freights. Double, triple and even quadruple-headed engines were used when lots of power was needed. In fact, the 4-6-0s and 2-8-0s were operated much like the GP and SD-series diesels of today as multiple units and for either passenger, freight or switching chores. The Locomotive Company's engines, Mantua's 4-6-0 and 4-8-0, MDC's "Old Time" 2-8-0 and 2-6-0, AHM's Casey Jones

4-6-0 and most of the HOn3, Sn3 and On3 locomotives are typical of this time period. All the LaBelle cars, MDC's truss-rod freight cars and cabooses, Central Valley kits and most narrow-gauge rolling stock date to this era.

THE TURN OF THE CENTURY

The real railroads began to assume their shape for the next forty years during the 1900–1915 period. Steel underframes were introduced to replace the truss rods and wood of earlier eras, but most of the boxcar, refrigerator car and caboose car bodies were still wood. Only the tank cars, hoppers, gondolas and flat cars were steel, and most of them had a profusion of rivets rather than the corrugations of later years. Cars like Life-Like's HO scale hoppers, gondolas and "wood" reefers are typical examples of what was modern then. The crack passenger trains were equipped with steel cars, and all but a few branch-line passenger cars had fully enclosed vestibules. The Athearn and AHM heavyweight passenger cars are typical, although the Athearn's are deliberately foreshortened versions of the more typical 80-foot cars, and

the wood cars were like MDC's and LaBelle's HO scale 80-footers. Freight trains were noteworthy for the tremendous variety of car lengths, from old truss-rod 32-footers with low roofs to tall and long 60-foot boxcars. A car like the wood-ended boxcars and reefers from Train Miniatures or Silver Streak in HO scale was about as modern as you could get in 1915.

The locomotives were much the same as during the Gay Nineties, but larger boilers and compound cylinders were common. The double-barreled look of the compound cylinders was pretty much unique to this period, for technological advances in steam efficiency made the easy-to-leak compound cylinders a thing of the past. The fast passenger trains like the Overland Limited and the Twentieth Century were pulled by Atlantics or Pacifics, while large—about as large as they came—consolidations and small Mikados did much of the freight hauling—still in double, triple or quadruple-headers, for the articulated locomotives were yet to come. The Locomotive Company is about the only builder of kits for compound locomotives, but there have been a few brass imports from this era for HO scale modelers.

Fig. 1-7 Consolidations (2-8-0s) and 10-wheelers (4-6-0s) were the most common types of locomotives in the 1890–1910 era, and most of the cars were still all-wood types with the exception of some steel hoppers and gondolas.

Fig. 1-8 The massive steam locomotives like this 2-10-4 bumped the smaller steam engines onto branch lines in the 1910–1940 period. The majority of the rolling stock was of steel construction.

THE ROARING TWENTIES

The period from about 1915 to 1934 was the heyday of the railroad in America. For most lines profits fell steadily from the end of World War I onward. 1929 marked the peak of railroad passenger travel in America. The United States Railroad Administration and the Association of American Railroads standardized, respectively, locomotive and freight car designs that were to remain almost unchanged through World War II. Really large steam locomotives like Mountains, Texas-types, Northerns and articulateds took over all the main-line operations, relegating the 10-wheelers and consolidations to local runs and branch lines. By 1934 the box cab diesel appeared and grew to a fleet of almost 300, and almost all different. Most new freight cars were steel with Dreadnaught and other types of corrugated steel ends similar to the Athearn HO scale cars, but the average car length was still about 40 feet in spite of many 50-foot boxcars, flat cars and gondolas. Most ca-

booses were steel, and the bay-window style was introduced on the B & O in 1931.

If you want to be accurate about your equipment for a period railroad scene from 1880 through 1945 or so, check the various *Train Shed 'Cyclopedias* published by Newton K. Gregg. These paperbacks are reprints of locomotive and rolling stock books of these eras that illustrate the current types of cars in, for example, the 1919 *Car Builders Dictionary* ('*Cyclopedias* number 35 and 36). The Bowser and Penn Line locomotive kits are typical HO scale examples of steam locomotive kits of this period.

THE END OF STEAM

Many model railroaders consider the period from 1935 to 1955 to be the best of all possible worlds to recreate in miniature. Streamline trains operated beside heavyweight steel cars from the twenties, 1900-era 10-wheelers and consolidations still chuffed along branch lines, while Southern Pacific cab-forward and Union Pacific Big Boy articu-

Fig. 1-9   Steam and diesel locomotives shared the head ends of America's trains in the 1940–1960 era. Most of the passenger trains were lightweight streamliners.

lateds pulled heavy freight trains. The almost-modern GP-7 and SD-7 hood-style diesels appeared, but the trim F-series cab diesels and delightful FA-1 and PA-1 Alco diesels handled the bulk of the better runs. Fifty-foot freight cars were more common than 40-footers, but longer cars were rare. For most,

these were the decades that marked the end of style in diesels as well as the end of steam. Each railroad had its own bright colors for its streamliners; some, like the SP and UP, had two or more combinations. Boxcars were still brown, reefers were still yellow and tank cars were still black, for the most part, with

Fig. 1-10   The 1960–1970 decade was one when most of the premerger railroads still retained their identity on their equipment, and passenger service was still part of each railroad's identity.

herals that dated back to the turn-of-the-century.

THE DAY OF THE DIESEL

The 1955–1975 decades are far more history, relative to the railroads, than you might guess (Fig. 1-10). Most of the changes that are standard today first appeared in the early seventies, but they didn't appear on more than a majority of the railroads' equipment until the last half of the decade of the seventies. There were few changes in the 1955–1965 period other than the complete disappearance of steam locomotives and the appearance of the hood-style diesels. The Electro-Motive SD-45 diesels that are typical of most of today's diesels first appeared in 1965. They represented a doubling of the horsepower of all the first-generation diesels, as well as a more squared-off styling. The always tall and often 80-foot long "hi-cube" cars appeared in the late sixties, and the TOFC (trailer on flat car) and COFC (container on flat car) cars appeared, first as 72-footers and later as 86-footers.

The mergers began in the seventies, but repainting was a slow process; so the modeler can elect to have, for example, green Burlington Northern diesels and cars as well as blue Great Northern equipment, red and grey Burlington diesels and cars, orange and green Northern Pacific diesels and all of the previous boxcar-red freight equipment and still have an authentic period railroad scene. If you like diesels, stop at about 1975 because the first-generation GP, SD, F-series, E-series, most Alcos and most G.E. diesels had all but vanished. You'll miss Conrail and most of the Railbox cars, and you can even skip Amtrak. If you want only modern equipment, then study the real thing, but do take a lot of photographs because the 1975–1985 decade is going to be as historical, some day, as 1900–1915 is today (Fig. 1-11).

Long locomotives and long cars can pose some real problems for a model railroader. The NMRA recommends a minimum 32-inch radius curve for HO scale (proportionally larger or smaller curves are needed for N, TT, S or O scales) for 80-foot passenger cars and 86-foot freight cars and for long-wheelbase steam locomotives like Texas-types and Northerns. Articulateds can negotiate tighter curves, but they look silly on anything smaller than a 27-inch curve (for HO scale). Passenger trains demand long sidings, then, as well as broad curves, unless you're willing to settle for older open-platform cars, Athearn's foreshortened heavyweights, or the

Fig. 1-11 80-foot freight cars, piggyback and container cars and a lack of roof walks mark most modern freight cars. Most railroads have similar caboose styles, and only the Rio Grande and Southern railroads maintain their own passenger car colors.

Athearn or Tyco "shorty" streamliners. When your freight trains require long sidings too, thanks to 86-foot hi-cubes and TOFC cars and 60-foot Railbox-style cars, you'll have to make some special concessions in your allotment of space for a layout. You can squeeze more life-like railroading into a smaller space by adopting a period prior to 1955, and you can do even more by going back to 1915 or earlier. Notice how many cars it takes to fill the small chunk of yard space in the photos, and you'll have an idea of how much space a modern-period model railroad can consume.

You will also need to be aware of periods if you choose to model narrow-gauge, traction or trolley lines. The Maine 2-foot narrow-gauge lines were abandoned by 1945, and the 3-foot narrow-gauge lines like the Rio Grande and East Broad Top became exclusively tourist lines by 1956. The turn of the century is generally considered the heyday of the Colorado narrow gauge, while the Maine lines and East Broad Top were at their peak in the period I call the twenties. The Maine 2-foot equipment still survives on the Edaville Railroad in South Carver, Massachusetts, but again it's strictly a tourist line. Two short stretches of the Colorado narrow gauge also live on as tourist-only operations in the seventies and with no rail connections to the outside world.

With the exception of some PCC-style cars from the fifties that operate on Boston, Philadelphia and Pittsburgh interurban lines, the trolleys have been gone from city streets since about 1955. If you want a trolley layout or to utilize trolleys in conjunction with regular railroading, you should pick one of the time periods from 1900 to 1955 for your layout. The selection of a definite time period is not quite as critical to the credibility of your layout as picking a constant scale for all the models, but it's almost that important. The compromise of bringing only certain periods' locomotives and rolling stock on stage can actually make your railroading more fun as well as more realistic. The period model railroad concept provides an excuse for the overabundance of locomotives and rolling stock that most of us seem to accumulate, by furnishing a showcase for just a portion of that equipment at any one time.

The four railroad empires on these pages represent what could only be called fulfilled dreams for their creators and operators. These are the kinds of model railroads that keep most of us interested in the hobby for a lifetime, always hoping that someday our layouts will look like those. Lonnie Shay is one of the top ten model railroaders in the world, Marshall Nelson has spent 20 years getting his layout to where it is today, and the other two are the work of clubs.

Try to set an attainable goal for your own model railroad. Be willing to spend 20 years if you have to have a large layout, or compromise and join a club to bring that date closer. If you're as good as Lonnie, you'll know it, and you won't need any more advice from us old-timers. There are other alternatives to a complete model railroad that might be the kind you'd really rather have. Take a look at the modular layouts in Chapter VI, and, if you're still in the imagination stage for that very first layout, look at the first two track plans in Chapter XII for examples of goals more easily attained.

THE ROCKY GORGE & SAINT ANNE RAILROAD

Marshall Nelson has taken what was the traditional approach to model railroading. In the wisdom of hindsight that comes after 20 years of model railroading, he readily admits that he would break with many of those traditions if he were to start a new layout today. I found his HO and HOn3 layout one of the finest I have ever seen. One of the best features of the line is that it's housed in its own room and that room is attached to the house (Fig. 2-1). Most model railroads that are as large as the Nelsons' are located in basements, attics or garages, areas that were not designed to be as habitable as the rest of the house. While we must make do with what we can get, the problems created by heat, cold, dust and humidity make the usual semihabitable locations a poor second choice. The major problem that faces any model railroad operator is electrical contact between the

Inspiration

always exposed railheads and the rolling metal wheels of the locomotives. Dust and humidity are the major factors that cause oxidation and a dirt buildup that electrically insulates the rails from the wheels.

You can avoid that problem by polishing the rails with a light abrasive pad (the Bright Boy is one good brand) and cleaning the wheels every month or so. The extremes of heat and cold cause the rails to expand and contract to loosen rail joiners and to play havoc with the tight tolerances around switches and crossings. The Nelson layout has few of those problems because, like the rest of the house, the layout room is heated in winter and air conditioned in the summer (and, not just incidentally, cleaned by Loretta Nelson along with the rest of her home).

Most of the trackage on this line is hand-spiked nickel silver rail laid on Campbell ties with a Homosote roadbed. The layout plan is a relatively simple two-lap loop with the upper loop set back about 3 feet from the table edge and the rear half of the lower loop hidden in a tunnel. A standard-gauge branch line leaves the main line on the upper level to terminate in a stub-end terminal on an extension of one corner of the layout. There is also a narrow-gauge branch line that runs more or less parallel to the standard-gauge tracks along the front of the table. Marshall plans to make this a full loop by adding a third rail to some of the standard gauge for some dual-gauge trackage through the lower loop's tunnel. All the switches are actuated by switch machines with built-in electrical contacts, so that by throwing the switch, power in or out of the siding or main lines into that switch is turned on or off—if the switch is thrown for the siding, then and only then will a locomotive on that siding operate. The system has made wiring the layout fairly simple with only a few toggle switches to control separate blocks. The branch line and the narrow-gauge line are each on their own control panels, so three trains can be operated at one time if desired.

The Nelson layout is built so the highest elevations—the branch-line yard and the upper loop to the rear of the layout—are just about at Marshall's shoulder level. The only way to get an overall view of the layout, or a photograph of all of it, is to stand on a ladder with your head touching the ceiling. The shoulder-level height forces you to look at the trains from virtually the same angle at which you would view the real thing, and the effect is most realistic. The layout room has one curved corner made with a piece of curved Masonite, which is plastered at the ends to blend with the rest of the wall. This provides a curved backdrop for a horizon without an alarming vertical seam. There is another 5 feet of room at one side of the layout and 10 feet or so at the other, so the layout room can also serve as a den. It's a tribute to Marshall's enthusiasm that he can have the family television set in the same room as the layout and still get any model railroading accomplished! The combination den/railroad room does, however, promote a certain togetherness that makes modeling more of a family hobby, even if the rest of the family elects to ignore the layout itself. Because the edge of

the layout is finished with a hardwood veneer, with a drape hiding the legs, the railroad has a finished look that makes it suitable for a den.

Everyone has some favorite aspect of the hobby, and for Marshall Nelson that is building construction from craftsman-type kits like Campbell, Fine Scale, Timberline, Dyna-Models, Suydam and SS Limited. Each of these structures has, however, been painted a

Fig. 2-1 Marshal Nelson's HO scale layout fills most of a 20 x 20-foot room attached to the Nelson home, so dust, temperature and humidity are easily controlled.

different color, or in the case of the Suydam two-story station, the siding and roof materials have been changed and the building has been reversed to put the freight end on the left. Two Revell plastic engine houses were joined, end to end, to build the branch-line engine house. A few of the structures have been scratch-built utilizing the same techniques as in the craftsman kits. Marshall has incorporated the best state-of-the-art ideas he could in the layout, but he has one regret: that the walk-in style layout design wasn't prevalent 20 years ago when he started the construction of this layout. When you con-

Fig. 2-2   The HOn3 engine house was scratch-built by Marshall Nelson using North-eastern-brand scale-size bass wood strips and milled sheets. The open-platform passenger cars in the foreground serve the branch line, while the steel cars like the double-door baggage travel the main line of the layout.

sider the amount of pleasure that the hobby has provided, that's not much of a mistake.

THE EAST VALLEY LINES

You could expect an N-scale club to be as modern as any, because N scale itself is just a bit more than a decade old. The northeast corner of the indoor exhibit area of Griffith Park, California's Traveltown is occupied by this 21 x 24-foot layout. The building is surrounded by Los Angeles's collection of about 15 full-scale steam locomotives along with about a dozen passenger cars, freight cars, cabooses, trolleys and a diesel-electric rail car. The club has chosen scenery typical of the higher mountain passes that surround Los Angeles, and one portion of the layout is detailed with rocks actually shaped like those on the Santa Susanna pass of the Southern Pacific Railroad. A full-scale model of the Los Angeles Union station is under construction for one corner of the layout. The layout has curves with a minimum radius of 30 inches (the equivalent of about 54 inches in HO scale!) so the typical 50-car freight looks most realistic as it sweeps around the hills.

The East Valley Lines is built on open-grid benchwork with Homosote for the roadbed base. The scenery is mostly Hydrocal plaster soaked into industrial paper towels with additional plaster rock carvings and rock castings for detail. There's a molded plaster dam on the partially completed side of the mountains. The club wisely chose a walk-in layout plan with walk-around throttle control. A master dispatcher sits on a platform above the layout, and the trains can be operated from that master panel. The system is the best of

Fig. 2-3 Mr. Nelson has effectively combined simple plastic kits like the Train Miniatures-brand section houses with craftsman-type kits like the Timberline water tower and Fine Scale sandhouse and coaling shed.

both worlds, for a club, because the train operators have their realistic rail-side view of their trains, and the dispatcher has his overall view. The controls are different than what you might expect, for the EVL is operated by a Fairchild microcomputer that controls the 30 separate power blocks and translates the signals from the push-button hand-held throttles. The microcomputer has no memory banks, so its programs must be recorded on cassettes. There's a keyboard so the programs can be changed or created right at the computer.

Felix Medak provided the computer, and Don Grodecki adapted it to the layout and designed the walk-around throttle controls. The blocks and the throttles can be operated manually if necessary. The walk-around throttles for the computer control have transistor control, of course, to provide the smoothest possible operation of the N-scale

locomotives. The club members accomplished what you see here in less than two years, and there's enough work in just the industrial and yard areas left to keep them busy for two more. In the meantime, the club is developing an operating schedule that will include both through freight and passenger trains as well as local trains and switching action.

Interestingly enough, N scale, even though it's one of the smallest scales, offers some distinct advantages for a club. N scale equipment is at its best in situations where four- to eight-unit diesels can pull 40- to 80-car freights just like the prototype. If you want to cram a lot of model railroading into a 2 x 4-foot space, then either choose one of the modular concepts from Chapter VI or build an HOn30" narrow-gauge railroad to the heftier HO scale with N-scale track, locomotive mechanisms, freight and passenger car

Fig. 2-4 The East Valley Lines N scale club layout features a walk-in design with the upper tracks at shoulder level. The partially completed scenery is formed from paper towels soaked in Hydrocal plaster.

trucks. The extreme light weight of the tiny N scale locomotives makes electrical contact and slow-speed control a problem for just one locomotive; when two or three locomotives can be operated together, there is always one to push or pull the other through the "stall" spots. A club, whether one with a permanent layout like the East Valley Lines or a portable NTRAK layout gathering, provides the long runs of trackage where N-scale equipment can really do what it does best, provide train-length operating scenes. Most of the N-scale locomotives and rolling stock are ready-to-run, and they're rugged. You can pack a four-unit diesel and 40 freight cars in a foam-padded briefcase for transportation to and from the club layout and keep just a few dioramas or a test track at home. Several of the East Valley Lines members have con-structed NTRAK modules in addition to helping with the club layout's construction and operation.

THE DY'N GLORY RAILROAD

There are masters in every field of endeavor including model railroading, and Lonnie Shay is one of them. His HOn3 layout incorporates just about everything that's best in the hobby, and Lonnie has executed those concepts perfectly. His layout is in a double-car garage, but it is walled off from the rest of the room, and particularly from the large door, into a space about 15 feet square. The arrangement provides him with ample space for a narrow-gauge layout in HO scale, while still leaving room for the usual nonautomotive uses of a garage as a workshop, laundry room, garden shop and storage shed. Too many model railroaders forget that they won't have any place to cut that lumber for the benchwork and scenery, for example, if they fill the garage with model railroad, or if they underestimate the social and humidity problems that an under-the-layout washer and dryer can present.

The arrangement also allows Lonnie to move the layout (it's built in bolt-together sections) into another garage without having to worry if the walls are 19 feet 6 inches or 18 feet 9 inches long. It's rather like having an island type of layout, but one with its own walls, and the concept would work just as well for a basement layout. If you keep one wall 18 feet or less and the other 12 to 15 feet, you should be able to relocate the layout in just about any basement *or* garage. The layout plan in Chapter XIII is one example of what can be fitted into a 13 x 18-foot space with HO scale or N scale equipment.

Lonnie's layout works because he has matched the scale of the equipment to the space available. Standard-gauge HO scale equipment would have demanded larger curves and a greater proportion of the scenery space in a 15-foot square room. N scale would work almost as well in his space, but the

Fig. 2-5   When an N scale layout is built in the space usually needed for HO scale, the curves can be almost as gentle as the prototype for realistic scenes like this one on the East Valley Lines layout.

Fig. 2-6   Paul Harris created this portion of the scenery on the East Valley Lines layout using a combination of latex rubber molds and hand-carving techniques to shape the rocks in Hydrocal and plaster of Paris.

curves are a bit tight for the 40-car freights that are the main advantage of N scale. HOn30″ or HOn2 equipment would have worked just as well, but Lonnie prefers the Rockies to the Maine environment of the real railroads that measured just 2 feet between the tops of the rails.

He worked out a loop-to-loop track plan similar to that in Chapter XII but with as much change in elevation as possible, and with a small town jutting out into the access aisle on its own peninsula. The end-of-track on the upper level is just a few inches below a

Fig. 2-7 The face and interior of one of the hand-held walk-around controllers Don Grodecki assembled for the East Valley Lines computer-controlled electrical system. The keyboard is part of the master computer terminal.

6-footer's eye level. With an exact-scale track plan, he was able to build open-grid benchwork with riser and track supports just where the track and structures would be and open areas in between. He used 3/16 x 1-inch "spine" lath strips placed on edge for his subbase, with 1/2-inch Homosote sliced (like the ties of flexible model railroad track) across the width of the roadbed to allow the Homosote to be curved to match the lath strips. He then filled the cracks in the Homosote with plaster. The result was a smooth-flowing track plan with "automatic" easements (transitions) from straight to curved track and between ess-bend curves. The actual plan of the track was altered a few fractions of an inch to place the risers and the trackwork over the Homosote and lath. The towns and some passing sidings are laid on a more conventional subbase of 1/2-inch plywood with 1/2-inch Homosote cut to fit. The trackwork utilizes individual ties with hand-spiked code 55 and code 70 rail and switches built to fit the flow of the trackwork. A PFM sound system provides both steam locomotive sound and track power. Mason Locomotive Works pushbutton-operated walk-around throttles are used with plug-in connectors at the two control panels.

The Shay perfection carries over to the scenery as well. Hydrocal and paper towels form the basic mountain shapes with the rock work cast in plaster from latex molds. The mountains dip almost 2 feet below the track and soar to the ceiling to effectively dwarf the HOn3 locomotives and rolling stock. The benchwork height was determined more by the depth of the canyons than by the level of the track. Lonnie pioneered the use of Caspia plants and ground foam for pine trees. He also uses pine-tree-shaped weeds for some of the trees and asparagus fern for some of the

Fig. 2-8 and 2-9 Lonnie Shay's HOn3 layout is a 15 x 15-foot masterpiece that features a long loop-to-loop plan with walk-in design and walk-around throttle control. The scenery is still in the raw plaster and paper towel stage along the rear wall.

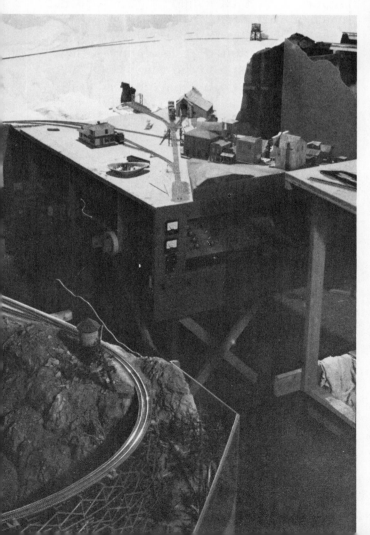

Fig. 2-10 The yards and industrial sidings are laid on sheets of Homosote with a plywood subbase on Lonnie Shay's layout. The rail is hand-spiked to individual ties.

branches to simulate three different types of pine trees.

The layout is currently in several stages of construction ranging from bare Homosote ready for ties to completed plaster mountains, and none of it is really finished. He plans to add a few more pine trees to the "finished" end of the layout and some epoxy resin water to the stream. The almost-completed scenery portion is another good idea incorporated into this layout, in that it allows him to pick and choose which aspect of the hobby he wants to do at any given time. Too many modelers insist on finishing all their trackwork before even beginning work on the scen-

Fig. 2-11 The tiny HOn3 locomotives are Far East Distributors' imports that Lonnie Shay has rebuilt with precision micromotors and gears and detailed with brass castings so they run as realistically as they appear.

ery, and as a result they don't do as good a job as they would if they had varied their modeling diet.

Knowing about the best type of layout design and benchwork, developing an even better system of roadbed support, and applying all these concepts to a layout design would be enough for most model railroaders, but Lonnie Shay's accomplishments don't stop there. There has always been a problem with operating model railroad equipment smaller than HO scale reliably at slow speeds. The HOn3, HOn2 and N-scale locomotives just don't weigh enough to break through the par-

ticles of dust and oxidation that can form even on just-cleaned track. The problem isn't quite so severe if the locomotives are traveling at a fairly high rate of speed so they coast over the rough spots—one reason why N scale locomotives are often geared for excessively high speeds. When you try to operate a single locomotive at the walking pace that is common for all switching on full-size railroads and for main-line operations on logging and narrow-gauge lines, then stalling locomotives can become a nightmare.

Lonnie was one of the first to fit the combination of ultralow gearing and a precision "can" motor or micromotor into a locomotive model. This gave his engines the slow speed and control he needed and helped to keep the motor's armature spinning even if there was a dead spot on the track. He then added small metal wipers to rub the track and more certain contacts for picking up and grounding the power. The results of his efforts are some of the finest-running locomotives in any scale, and he went on from there to equip the tiny engines with PFM sound systems. He has matched the locomotives' gearing so that most run at almost the same speed for double-heading operation. His locomotives, however, unlike most ready-to-run N, HOn30" or HOn3 engines, do not have to be double-headed just so one can push or pull the other over the stall spots.

THE HIGHLAND PACIFIC

This HO scale railroad is one that fulfills just about any model railroader's dream of the ultimate. The railroad is housed in its own 40 x 42-foot building plus a one-bedroom house to provide separate rooms for woodworking, model building and library. The two structures are air conditioned and heated. The ceiling of the layout room is about 20 feet high to allow enough room for an operating balcony that overlooks the layout. This, of course, is the type of layout that could only be constructed with the pooling of labor and skill that exists in the better model railroad clubs. This is actually the second empire that the

Highland Park Society of Model Railroad Engineers has created. The first layout was located in the basement of a hobby shop in Highland Park, California, and was started in 1948.

The club was forced to move in 1959, and the members spent the next three years searching for a piece of property where no further moves would ever be necessary. The present location in San Gabriel was purchased in 1962, and the house served as an office and workshop while the layout building was being constructed. Stan Garner, an expert welder and contractor, did most of the building construction, and he is the one responsible for the layout's unusual welded steel-tube benchwork. A club layout this large has to be strong enough to walk on for major construction and maintenance projects. That means extra-heavy scenery and supports. The steel benchwork makes the layout as strong as the building itself.

The majority of the Highland Pacific Railroad is built along conventional lines with 1 x 4s and ½-inch plywood for most of the subbase and Homosote roadbed. The trackwork is code 100 nickel silver rail on individual wood ties. The switch machines are a rotary style bought by the gross from a surplus store. The electrical wiring is carried in metal-covered troughs in the cement floor to a central terminal bank. All of the relays that control the blocks and signals are in a series of cabinets along one wall. The principal means of train control are three master panels, complete with track diagrams, on the elevated control platform. Illuminated strips show which blocks the dispatcher has assigned to each engineer for the route of his train out of the yards and through the passing sidings on the main line. The dispatcher's control panel actuates all of the track switches, and the engineers have control over the track blocks. There is a provision for track-side control for yard and peddler freight switching operations.

The 20-foot-long passenger yard and an equal length freight yard are the activity

Fig. 2-12   The rock work on Mr. Shay's layout is plaster cast in latex rubber molds he lifted from real rocks.

centers of the layout. These areas are nearly complete, while the other two-thirds of the layout is under various stages of construction, ranging from finished scenery supports to bare Homosote sites for the sidings and the yet-to-come HOn3 logging line on the east half of the layout. The track plan is basically point-to-point with the giant passenger and freight terminal on one end and a "fiddle" yard and reverse loop at the other. It takes a freight train traveling at about a scale 25-miles-an-hour almost a half-hour to travel over the layout. The curves are broad enough so that 80-foot passenger cars and 86-foot

Fig. 2-13 The Highland Park Society of Model Railroad Engineers has constructed one of the largest HO scale layouts in the country. This is only about one-third of the 40 x 42-foot empire.

TOFC or piggyback TrailerTrain cars can be operated in 40-car and longer trains. The club meets on Wednesday evenings. It designates one evening a month for operation and three for construction and maintenance. Each member has his own key so he can build in the shop or work on the layout or operate whenever he wishes.

Fig. 2-14 Plywood formers and cloth shape the mountains on the Highland Park club's layout, with the final surface a thick coat of Hydrocal-soaked paper towels.

Fig. 2-15 The industrial portion of the Highland Park layout has been detailed with cast plaster retaining walls and scratch-built industrial buildings to represent an eastern city. Van Facko did most of this work.

Fig. 2-16   An industrial area helps to hide the transition from city to mountains on the Highland Park layout. The three corrugated structures are Suydam-brand all-metal kits.

Fig. 2-17   The Highland Park club's layout designers made effective use of the space to fit broad-radius curves that are not practical on smaller home layouts.

Locomotive Conversions

The locomotives are the superstars of any model railroad layout. You can spend a year's worth of weekends finishing a contest-winning station with a full interior and working door locks, but it will be what's at the head end of those trains that everyone will notice. The painting and detailing of locomotives has become almost a hobby within the hobby. The trend toward adding that custom touch to a locomotive began with steam engines like the HO scale Mantua, Bowser, Penn Line and MDC models that needed some Kemtron, CalScale, Cary or Precision cast brass detail parts to look as good as those imported brass ready-built engines. Now firms like Utah Pacific, Detail Associates, Details West and Holgate and Reynolds make the small vents and louvers and spark arrestors and snow plows and the countless other items that make one real railroad's diesels different from another's. The availability today of both steam and diesel locomotive detailing parts and the development of airbrush weathering has made the model locomotive a miniature worthy of the attention it receives.

DIESEL LOCOMOTIVES

For the newcomer, the differences in diesels are hard to spot. It's difficult to tell a GP-7 from a GP-9, let alone why the SantaFe's GP-9 might be different from the Union Pacific's. If you are modeling a specific prototype railroad, then the details might be very important. If you merely need motive power for your own line, then you can establish your railroad's own variations on the stock diesels. You may decide that all of your diesels should have Holgate and Reynolds snow plows, like most Southern Pacific units, or, like the Maryland & Pennsylvania, that your diesels should be fitted with the type of pilots once used on steam locomotives. You might also standardize on just one type of spark arrestor for your diesel switchers. Each real railroad often has its own "standard" diesel headlight, and that too is a detail that gives a realistic family look to your diesels. All of these parts are available as plastic or metal castings in HO scale, and some are offered in O scale. Use photographs you take yourself, photographs from magazines and books like Kalmbach's *Diesel Spotters Guide* to determine what details you might wish to add to your diesel locomotives.

There are some details that should be applied to any HO scale diesel. The hand rails supplied with Athearn's diesels are as fine as you can buy and a noticeable improvement over the rather heavy plastic railings on all other brands of plastic-bodied diesels. You can buy the hand rails as separate kits from many model railroad dealers. Find an Athearn diesel that's similar to the one you want to detail and purchase the hand-rail kit for it—you may have to bend the hand rails themselves from .020-inch-steel piano wire to adapt the kit to your model. The stamped-metal hand-rail posts in the Athearn diesel kits and in their hand-rail kits are as near to scale as you can get. The vast opening in the ends of most diesels' pilots should be filled, in part, with Kadee couplers mounted on the frame of the diesel rather than on the pivoting trucks. Fill in around the coupler with scraps

Fig. 3-1 David Werner superdetailed this Athearn HO scale SD-45 diesel to match the features unique to the full-size Pennsylvania locomotives in premerger days.

of plastic, and bend a simulated coupler lift bar from .015-inch steel wire. Use some single strands of common household lamp-cord wire to simulate the rings that hold the coupler lift bars on the ends of a full-size diesel. Finish the details with some Kemtron, Precision, CalScale or Detail Associates air hoses to simulate the "mu" connections (the control and brake connections that allow one engineer and fireman to control two or more diesel locomotives). If your model doesn't have end steps, then make some from .030-inch styrene sheet or use one of the Holgate and Reynolds or Details West snow-plow pilots.

There are dozens of tiny details like the lift rings on the top of real diesels, special air horns, speedometer cables or shock absorbers on trucks, fuel tank fillers, end steps, chains, etc., etc., that can also be added to your model to give it that cluttered look that is only apparent when you look closely at a full-size

diesel. You might also want to remove any cast-on hand rails or grab irons and replace them with pieces of bent .010-inch wire. Fabricate windshield wipers from the same material painted black for the blade and aluminum for the wiper arms. There are subtle grill, vent, and stack changes that make a conversion from, say, a GP-9 to a GP-7 the matter of just a few hours' fun.

Few of the ready-to-run diesels are painted or lettered neatly enough to satisfy most model railroaders. If you decide to reletter your diesels, you should try to remove the factory paint with Scalecoat's paint remover, automobile brake fluid or one of the ultrasonic cleaning machines. Be sure to test a sample of any paint remover on the bare plastic inside the body to see if the fluid attacks the plastic. Once the diesel is painted (as described in Volume I of the *Model Railroading Handbook*), apply the railroad lettering decals of your choice and the tiny letters like "fuel

Fig. 3-2 Each of David Werner's Pennsylvania diesels is a replica of one of the real railroad's actual diesels: (from l to r) an Athearn SD-45, an AHM U25C, an Alco Models U25B, an Athearn GP-35, an Alco SD-40 and an Alco C630.

capacity" from one of the Micro Scale diesel decal sheets.

STEAM LOCOMOTIVES

There was a day, in the sixties, when you might have considered modifying a brass ready-built steam locomotive. Today, though, that imported brass locomotive that sold for $65 in 1965 may be worth as much as $300 in its unpainted original form—if modified, it might be worth one-fifth that. That's one reason why many steam-era modelers are modifying relatively inexpensive kits rather than the brass imports. Mantua and MDC locomotives are inexpensive enough to allow you to purchase an entire engine just to get the chassis or superstructure. Some of the AHM, Life-Like, Bachmann and Model Power locomotives with the small "RP-25"-size wheel and driver flanges can also provide chassis for particular conversions. Penn Line and Bowser locomotive chassis are also available separately, as are the Locomotive Company's 2-8-0 and 4-6-0 series of chassis. The Locomotive Company superstructures are packaged as separate kits, Cary makes conversion boilers, and Bowser, Penn Line, MDC and AHM superstructure parts are available separately.

Fig. 3-3 Each railroad has some feature that marks its diesels as being different from all other railroads. The side rails and spark arrestors on this NW-2 are as necessary as the paint and lettering to duplicate number 81 in miniature.

Most of these firms also offer individual tender kits, or at worst, you can order the parts to build any of their tenders direct from them. Kemtron makes a brass mogul, and Keystone has nice cast-metal Shay. All of these kits are HO scale; there are a few inexpensive O scale kits and some N scale conversion parts available from smaller manufacturers from time to time. Kemtron and Precision do make some superdetailed O scale and On3 all-brass solder-together locomotive kits that sell for about the same price as some brass imports.

The Kemtron, Precision, CalScale, Cary and Back Shop brass detail parts are just the ticket for adding extra and necessary details to steam locomotive conversions. Most of these parts were made for the solder-together kits or to be used as the details on some of the imported brass locomotives. The parts are small enough, however, that they can be attached to any of the plastic or metal models with a dab of five-minute epoxy.

Steam locomotives had more visible details than diesels, and there was a greater variety of sizes, styles and shapes. You probably have spotted a few favorites already, and more will be discovered when you begin to do some research by reading books on real steam-era railroading. You could, for one example, build an almost perfect HO scale replica of the Maryland & Pennsylvania Railroad's number 26 consolidation shown in Chapter XI using commercial components and parts. A Locomotive Company number 22 consolidation chassis would provide the correct chassis. MDC's number 81600 Old Timer boiler is perfect, but it will have to be cut in half just behind the rear (steam) dome so the metal can be removed from inside the boiler to clear the Locomotive Company chassis's "can" motor. Kemtron's number 267 Ma

Fig. 3-4   The Ma & Pa is one of the few real railroads to have fitted steam locomotive style pilots to its diesels like that on this SW-9. It has a switching pole and rerail frog hung from its side that also date back to the days of steam.

& Pa cab is just right with a Kemtron 302 stack and Kemtron or CalScale's compressor, bell, whistle, headlight and pop valves. MDC's number 404 Old Timer tender is also perfect. The product of this combination of parts would look at least as good as the best of the imports of number 26, it would run better than any of them, and it would cost about two-thirds to three-fourths as much.

There are countless other chassis, superstructure, tender and detail parts combinations that will produce equally successful steam locomotives. You may have to search the manufacturers' catalogs and the books on the prototypes to find combinations of kit parts to match the prototypes, but it's a really enjoyable experience just searching for a few favorites. Creating and operating the locomo-

tive you know is yours alone is even more fun than putting it together.

THE ART OF AIRBRUSHING

The finely ground pigments in paints like Floquil and Scalecoat produce such a thin coat of paint that application by brush is a practical proposition. It's also possible to "weather" a steam locomotive or diesel with a paintbrush or an aerosol can, but believe me, it's a difficult job. The airbrush, a type of model-size spray gun, is one of those tools that can produce almost magical results for even a beginning modeler.

The cost of purchasing a complete airbrush outfit is somewhat less than it used to be

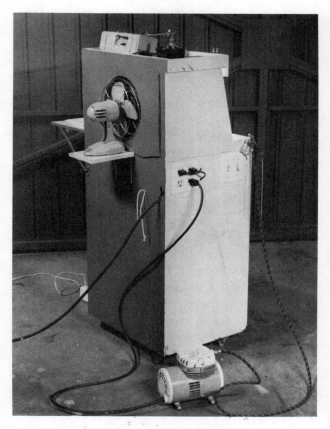

Fig. 3-5   Larry Larson converted a kitchen cabinet into a portable spray-painting booth. The fan pulls the air and the paint fumes through a replaceable furnace filter.

Fig. 3-6   The compressor is usually stored inside the cabinet with the paints. The cabinet has its own built-in fluorescent light and plugs for the compressor or additional lights.

because several firms are making special airbrushes just for modelers, and because the cost of the air compressors has been reduced slightly. A professional-quality airbrush like a Badger 150, Binks, Paasche, or Thayer and Chandler unit will still run over $60. Badger, however, has introduced a hobby version of their airbrush series that has an adjustable spray. Their model 350 sells for about $20. You will have to add either a pressure regulator and spray cans (about $7) or one of the $80 air compressors sold by Badger, Sears and others. Badger also makes a $1.25 adapter to mount its spray can regulator on an automobile or truck tire's inner tube. The problem with spraying with an air supply from an inner tube is that the air pressure will become lower as the air is depleted. With practice, you can press on the inner tube with your

foot to keep the air pressure reasonably steady. There's really no substitute for a good air compressor. You should be prepared to add another $30 to the cost of the compressor for one of the combination water traps, pressure regulators and gauges to get the most out of any airbrush—in all, consider an air brush to be a $130–$150 investment that can be purchased in stages. Learn the art of airbrushing by practicing the weathering effects.

The airbrush can hide a world of mistakes and make a $2 plastic ready-built model look like a $20 craftsman kit by shading and weathering the cheap model so its shortcomings are only apparent to an expert. A fine coat of flat or matte-finish Scalecoat or Floquil paint will show up every mold line, every glue joint, and every oversize rivet and grab iron on any model. A correct application of decals (as

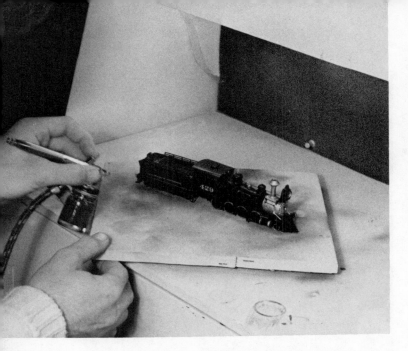

Fig. 3-7 A board, bolted to a pivoting lazy susan, serves as the platform for spray painting so most models can be painted on three of their four sides by simply turning the platform.

visible. Properly applied weathering duplicates the cloudlike puffs of dirt and the rain-washed dribbles of dirt that appear on almost every real-life building, locomotive or freight car.

The weathering that I'm referring to is a wash that consists of about five parts paint and 95 parts thinner. It's possible to dab this wash onto a model with a piece of cotton, a piece of fine-pore sponge or just the tip of a number 1 or 2-size paint brush, but the effect will not be quite as realistic as the same pattern would be if applied with an airbrush. The airbrush can be moved and the spray stopped to feather or blend the edge so it's almost impossible to see where the weathering spot ends and the clean surface begins. The dabbing with the wash of mostly thinner can loosen and soften paint or decals too, which would not be affected by the air brush.

The one secret to effective weathering with an airbrush is to keep the spray pattern and the distance from the airbrush to the surface in a balance that allows only the barest trace of paint to reach the model, with that paint

shown in Volume I), will help to pull the viewer's eye from some of the model's faults and a thin coat of light grey or beige weathering will make most of those flaws almost in-

Fig. 3-8 Locomotives or cars that are to be lettered with decals should be given a coat of gloss to help the decal adhere, followed by an additional coat of matte or flat-finish clear paint and some degree of weathering. This is Badger's model 350 airbrush.

barely wet when it lands. You are almost literally "dusting" the weathering wash onto the model with the airbrush, so there will be little chance of softening decals or dissolving the original color coats on the model's surface. The combination of the slight color proportion in the wash and the light application in the dusting spray will also make it difficult to get too much weathering on the model. Try a first coat over the lower edges of the model and the roof—the places where the most dirt collects on almost any building, locomotive or freight car—and step back to see how you like the effect. That one light coat will be enough for equipment that has "just left the paint shop." Apply a second coat to the next model you weather for that more-typical year old or so appearance. A very few models should receive some additional weathering coats and perhaps even some special stains and runs to simulate unusual dirt or commodity-spillage conditions.

Decide on a geographic locale for your railroad and find out what the predominant earth color is in that area. Only a few farming areas have brown dirt; most have boxcar red, beige or dark grey (but NOT black). The color of the local earth is blown over everything in that area and dissolved into the very pores of the wood, bricks and stone and the paint's oxidized surfaces. For really life-duplicating models, then, everything on your model railroad should get at least a single dust-on application of the proper wash of color and thinner from an air brush. Older cars and structures should get additional coats plus some light grey wash to fade out the colors in the manner that the sun fades them in real life. You could spot the terminus of a railroad in the steam locomotive era by the dark grey cast on most of the buildings, and today you can spot coal-mining areas in the same manner. Iron-mining towns have a boxcar red hue, and desert towns have a beige coloration. Remember to spray at least a trace of that same color over the trackwork, rocks, and other scenic details when they are completed (even leaves and grass get a light coating of dust in real life).

Your locomotives and rolling stock should

Fig. 3-9   Highlight wooden surfaces like the tops of toolboxes, running boards and tender floors on older-era steam locomotives with a dry-brush touch of beige to accent the wood grain.

Fig. 3-10   The same stains that collect on the inside of a water pot or automobile radiator used to collect around the steam whistles and pop valves on steam locomotives' steam domes. Use tiny dabs of light grey flat-finish paint to simulate the stains.

present some weathering contrasts to the overall colors on the layout. Both steam and diesel locomotives should be weathered with dark grey along the top surfaces—the wheels, drivers and trucks should get a touch of the local earth color. Hoppers, gondolas and other coal-carrying cars should get that same almost-black treatment; grain-carrying covered hoppers and boxcars should receive a light beige weathering, cement and chemical carrying cars a light grey touch. Remember to touch the tops of tunnel portals, overpasses, and track-side roofs with a dark grey weathering coat too. One point of caution about weathering or any other kind of model painting; be sure to apply the paint under lighting conditions identical to those on your model railroad. If your layout is illuminated by fluorescent lights, then be sure the area where you paint has the same type of lighting. Above all, don't paint outdoors (unless of course you're actually building an outdoor railroad) because colors in the sun are just not the same as colors under artificial light. Colors even change their value or their appearance when viewed under incandescent lights versus fluorescent lights.

When you have developed a feeling for the controls and operation of your airbrush by applying weathering coats, you can use that experience in applying color coats to paint or in repainting your models. The smaller air

Fig. 3-11 Diesels, like this repainted and decaled N scale set, are much more realistic with a light touch of dark grey weathering on the tops and some dirt-colored beige along the trucks and fuel tanks.

compressors and aerosol cans like Badger's Propel usually develop something less than 25 psi (pounds per square inch) of air pressure. If you use a larger compressor, then adjust its pressure regulator down to 40 psi or less for applying matte finishes and down to about 20 psi for spraying gloss finishes. Adjust the airbrush's paint-flow nozzle, and if necessary the air pressure at the compressor, so you can hold the airbrush about 4 to 6 inches from the model's surface without having the paint splatter from too much force or dry before it reaches the surface. Always hold the nozzle perpendicular to the surface you are painting by turning the model or angling it as needed. Start the spray off the model and pass the paint pattern smoothly and evenly over the model and beyond before releasing the spray button. If the paint runs, you are likely holding the airbrush over the model for too long a time (try quicker strokes across the model's surface), or you are holding the brush too close to the model. It's one of those learn-by-doing techniques; those are the basics you'll need to know so you can correct your own mistakes.

ADVANCED CROSS-KITTING TECHNIQUES

The locomotive kits produced by firms like Kemtron and Precision are superbly detailed miniatures with virtually all of the components cast in brass. It's possible to assemble these models with epoxy or the cyanoacrylate cements like Eastman 910, but they are really intended to be soldered together. There are some interim projects in which you can attempt to learn the soldering techniques and learn whether or not you want to attempt one of these advanced locomotive kits: The Suydam corrugated metal structure kits are designed for solder-together construction, and each kit includes a small pamphlet on the basics of soldering. The tolerances on these buildings are not as critical as they are on a locomotive model, so there's more room for the mistakes you can make while learning. You might also try a single brass component,

Fig. 3-12 This On30″ Forney is an example of the craftsman type of steam locomotive conversions. The complete chassis is a stock Tyco 0-4-0 ready-to-run with Bob Sloan's etched brass superstructure.

like the Kemtron Ma & Pa cab assembly (the pieces are all brass) suggested earlier in this chapter. Bob Sloan also makes a number of cabs and tender bodies for most of the Colorado narrow-gauge lines and for the Colorado Midland standard gauge in HO, S and O scales that should be soldered together. Sloan makes an inexpensive all-brass Forney locomotive kit in HO and O scale (for HOn2, HOn30″, HOn3, On2 or On3 gauges depending on which type of chassis and truck you use). The design of the Forney is similar to those used on the Maine 2-foot gauge

railroads. It's the type of a small locomotive that can be customized or freelanced into a backwoods design for your own railroad (or for a narrow-gauge branch line to connect with your standard-gauge line), so the exact details and even the fit of some of the parts can be a little "strange" and the model will still look just fine. The construction of a cab or tender or a simple locomotive like the Forney (over an HO chassis for On2 or an N scale one for HOn30″) will give you the experience you need to decide whether or not you are ready for a complete solder-together locomotive kit.

Rolling Stock

Freight and passenger cars are only a part of the overall mixture of models that will make your layout look like either a railroad in miniature or just another toy train. It may seem a bit silly to consider the visitor's impression of your model railroad; you, after all, are the only one who really should be pleased. When you are the one that buys and builds all of that equipment, though, it's far too easy to fall into the can't-see-the-forest-for-the-trees trap. I've suggested that you tone down the overall appearance of your entire layout with some of the weathering colors that Mother Nature uses on the outside world, because out-of-the-box models have finishes that are far too bright to look real, regardless of how accurate the details may be. Most of the photos you'll see on these pages deal with how to make a specific piece of your miniature empire seem more like the real thing. There are too few that give the overall feeling that's necessary to achieve a model railroad as realistic as, for example, Lonnie Shay's. The mixture of rolling stock models can have a far

greater effect on the realism of your railroad than individual grab irons on the cars.

Most of us purchase the models we do—either as ready-builts, kits, or parts and "scratch" to build our own—because there is some particular appeal about that particular model or prototype. Some of us may go so far as to select a real railroad and limit our purchases to locomotives, cars and structures that would (or did) appear on that prototype, but even those are choices that we desire to make. The real railroads aren't lucky enough to be able to have the rolling stock that they want; they have to have pretty much what they need in order to come even close to making a profit. One of the ways they fill that need is by doing something that is a shocking consideration to most model railroaders; the real railroads buy more than one—many more—of everything. Have you ever even thought about buying 10 or 20 of just one type of boxcar with just one road name? If you haven't, then your model railroad is lacking one essential ingredient of realism; it's not dull enough due to a lack of identical cars.

There are so many choices confronting you when you enter a hobby shop that a choice of 10 items is highly unlikely to end up being a choice of 10 of the same thing. Ten identical boxcars can, however, do more to make your railroad more realistic than 20 different diesels or 20 different reefers. There are certain trade-offs you must make in this hobby. One of them is whether you want your freight cars to look like a collection of circus-colored cars with no two the same color or shape, or if you want your freight cars to at least look as if they do what they're supposed to—make a profit for your railroad.

The best way to avoid the no-two-cars-alike pitfall is to establish some kind of goal for the total number of freight and passenger cars you intend to have in, say, a year, in 3 years, when your layout's trackwork is all complete, etc., etc. One of your other goals is going to be that of creating some type of realistic railroad, and part of that goal will be to decide which prototype you are going to duplicate or which prototype you will more or less match with your "Basement & Bedboard Central."

Fig. 4-1   There's a definite toylike translucence about an unpainted plastic model, and a heavy feeling around the ladders and grab irons and steps.

Fig. 4-2   A genuine wooden roof walk, individual grab irons and steps, paint and decal lettering can make even the least expensive plastic model look as if it was assembled from one of the craftsman kits.

One of the characteristics of the prototype for your railroad will be what types of freight and passenger cars it uses, why, and how many. The geographic setting for your railroad can also play an important part in the assortment of car types; there would obviously be more hopper cars in sight on a mountain railroad in a mining district than on a line through Iowa.

You may even have chosen the prototype for your railroad based on the fact that you liked the types of cars that ran on that real railroad. Some modelers build their entire layout around the vision of seeing a 40-car train of Pacific Fruit Express reefers in operation or long drags of dirty hoppers snaking around the mountains. If you're one of those, then you're closer to accomplishing that goal of building a realistic railroad than most, because your dream happens to correspond with reality. The one thing that no real railroad has is a totally different mixture of rolling stock like that usually seen on a model railroad. Even a train that appears at first to be made up of a string of cars, with no two alike, will probably have at least a dozen cars of the same type and size and markings mixed at random into the consist.

There is no possible way for even a club to match the exact proportions of cars that appear on most real railroads; if they did, they would probably only have three cabooses on the entire railroad. Your trains will be shorter than the prototype's, so you'll have to have more cabooses than might be strictly correct. That same short-train reality can allow you to have relatively fewer cars lettered for your home railroad than occurs on the prototype, for the simple reason that you're going to have fewer cars per locomotive (you'll also have, of course, a greater proportion of locomotives as compared to cars).

Let's consider a hypothetical example of a model railroad with a goal of 40 freight cars. The average train length will likely be about six cars on a railroad that size, so you can figure that there will be enough cars for seven trains with five left over for cabooses and work cars. Only about half of those 35 freight cars should ever be in a train at a given time; the rest should be on industrial sidings or in the yards, so three to five cabooses and a few work cars should be plenty. Right here is one problem of discipline; limiting yourself to just five cabooses or to just a few work cars.

An average real railroad will be assembled from about half its own cars and half cars from some other line. The major exceptions to that rule are lines that carry only "bridge" traffic between two other connecting railroads and railroads that only operate, for example,

hopper cars around mining areas. The bridge line will have few cars of its own, however; half of its traffic will be cars lettered for one or the other of the two connecting roads. The all-hopper line would have only a few cars from other railroads. The cars for other railroads— 17 of them, in this model railroad example— can be just about anything you want, and there don't have to be two of anything in that assortment.

The 18 cars for your home line should be divided into groups or sets of identical cars with a few leftovers; six boxcars, six hoppers, three reefers, a gondola, a flat car, and a tank car would be one very typical assortment. To give a hint of the appearance of a real railroad, at least four of those boxcars, four of the hoppers and two of the reefers should be identical cars except for their car numbers and the degree of weathering. If your railroad is patterned after the operations of one that hauls a lot of fruit, then swap the quantities for hoppers and reefers. If you're modeling a coal-hauling railroad, then at least double the number of hoppers and select two boxcars and one reefer.

One of the goals of this exercise in a 40-car model railroad is to at least enable you to make up an occasional solid (five cars plus caboose) train of home cars and still have one or two left over to be on a siding or in another train. The mixture of "foreign" railroads' rolling stock that travels over your railroad is very likely going to be in about the same proportions as your own equipment. In reality, the proportions of flat cars, gondolas and tank cars is usually less than I've suggested, but it's nice to see such unusual rolling stock at least lettered for the predominant railroad in the area.

The real railroads often operate solid trains of flat cars, particularly the 86-foot TOFC or piggyback types with trailers or containers on them. If your railroad is set in a modern era and serves a seaport, then you might want to substitute those flat cars for hoppers. The point is that out of 18 cars lettered for your favorite railroad, two batches of four and a batch of two should be identical in every respect except for numbers and weathering, if

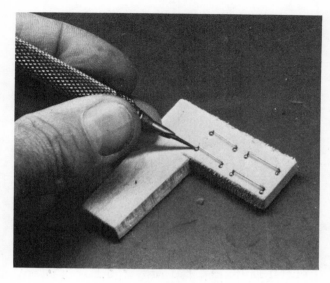

Fig. 4-3 For an extra touch of realism drill a second hole next to each end of the grab irons and insert a small pin or one of the Grandt-brand nut-bolt-washer castings.

you expect to capture the feeling and appearance of real railroading. When you're buying that next car on impulse, try to collect enough willpower to save some funds for a set of four

identical cars. There is a bonus to this system; you'll discover that a train of identical cars appears to be much longer than one with a variety of rolling stock in it. The layout planning concepts in Chapters XI and XIII might help to clarify the need for the correct mixture of equipment on some specific model railroads. Be careful too that you keep your cars in the correct time period including those in the foreign road grouping.

CONVERSIONS AND CROSS-KITS

A conversion can be as simple a matter as removing the lettering from a boxcar with Scalecoat paint remover, or in some cases with 70-percent solutions of isopropyl alcohol and relettering the car for your home railroad with decals or dry transfers. A conversion can add enough details to an inexpensive plastic car to make it look like a craftsman kit, and a conversion can be as complex as grafting two different model cars together to create a third

Fig. 4-4 Grab iron detail is most obvious on a light-colored car where the hardware was painted boxcar red or roof brown to match the sides, roof and ends of the prototype.

one that is not available any other way. If you are going to go to the trouble of repainting a model, then you might as well take another evening and replace some of the bulkier details with items that are more in scale with the rest of the car. Most of the plastic kit and ready-built cars in HO and O scales have molded-on ladders, grab irons, steps and too-thick molded plastic roof walks. These items are easy enough to remove with a hobby knife, and new wire parts require some easy-to-drill holes to match the wire diameter. A wood roof walk can simply be glued in place with Goodyear Pliobond or Walthers Goo cement. LaBelle strip brass steps can be used to replace the plastic steps, or you can just whit-

tle the stock steps to a more realistic thickness. If the couplers are not mounted on the body, then by all means mount a pair of Kadees there.

There are hundreds of freight and passenger car conversions that are possible by cutting plastic freight and passenger car bodies in half. With some careful cuts, you can make a full baggage car from two AHM 80-foot baggage/coach cars—use the leftover pieces with some of Walthers metal sides to make a full postal car of the same heavyweight era. The MDC HO scale Harriman cars are models of prototypes that were once standard on the Southern Pacific, Union Pacific and Illinois Central railroads, but only the baggage and

Fig. 4-5 Marshall Nelson spliced two Athearn 50-foot gondola bodies together to produce this 60-foot car. This gondola, like the Athearn 40-foot tank car and the MDC tanks cars in the foreground, has been repainted and lettered with decals, then lightly weathered.

postal cars are the correct length. Splice the long halves from two coaches, two observations or a coach and a diner to make the correct-length 80-foot coach, observation and diner cars. The 34-foot MDC open-platform passenger cars make nice 60-foot cars when two of them are cut and spliced into a single car. Be sure, by the way, to replace the trucks on those longer Harriman cars with six-wheel trucks and to fit MDC, Central Valley or Walthers old-time passenger-car trucks to the longer open-platform cars. The same techniques can, of course, be used to make scale-length models of the too-short Athearn heavyweight and streamlined cars.

The basic cutting and fitting operations are simple enough; cut each body with an X-Acto razor saw, sand the cut ends so they fit snugly against each other, and glue them with Testors' liquid cement for plastics. The trick is to make the saw cuts about 1/32-inch away from where you want the final joint to leave yourself some "fiddle" room to get the fit just right. Trick number two is to use plenty of glue and press the cut parts together tightly enough so that a small bead of cement-softened plastic oozes out of the seam. Let that seam dry for a day or two, then carefully slice the bead away, and you may not even have to use body filler to hide the seam. If that ploy still leaves a visible seam, then use automobile metal-base auto-body putty or Micro-Scale's Silver putty for models to fill in the seam. Let the putty dry for another day or two and sand it smooth with number 600 wet-or-dry sandpaper dipped in water so it won't scratch the plastic. Wash the model in detergent and rinse with warm water, then dry it in the air—no rag-wipes to leave lint. Spray a coat of primer or flat black over the model to see if the seam shows, and if necessary, use more putty to completely fill the seam. When the fit is perfect, apply the final coat of paint and decals.

SHOP-STYLE CAR CONSTRUCTION

The full-size car-building shops seldom assembled one car at a time, and there's no

Fig. 4-6 Carefully scribe the line where you want to cut the plastic, then saw 1/32-inch to the "scrap" side of the line with an X-Acto razor saw to leave material for file-to-fit assembly.

Fig. 4-7 Hold a piece of fine-grit sandpaper on a plate of glass and rub the part back and forth on the sandpaper to give the final flush-fit to the joints between two pieces of plastic.

reason why you should either. You can adopt the same all-wood construction techniques used for Ambroid, Quality Craft, LaBelle Woodworking, Scotia, Central Valley or Camino kits to build those wood-style boxcars, reefers, flat cars, or gondolas a half-dozen or a

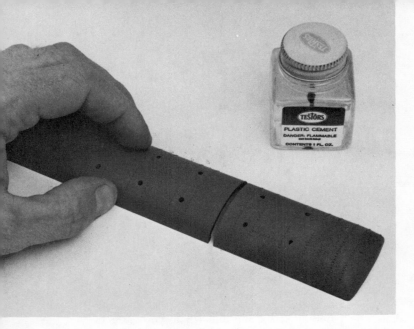

Fig. 4-8 When you're joining two pieces of a plastic car back together, to produce a longer or shorter car, use Testor's *liquid* plastic cement rather than any of the cements in a tube.

Fig. 4-9 Wrap some 400-grit wet or dry sandpaper over a scrap of wood or a doctor's tongue depressor to sand the cemented joint smooth after the glue has dried for at least 24 hours.

dozen at a time. You might be surprised to learn that you really are not likely to save any money this way—the cost of the materials, cast detail parts, grab irons, decals, trucks and couplers will just about equal the cost of using kits for the same number of cars. You can, however, produce a slightly different set

of equipment with, for example, a roof line a scale foot lower than any of the kits to make your efforts notable.

If you just want to save time, then buy a half-dozen or a dozen kits and build them all at once. The construction time can often be cut in half by completing all of the various stages at one time. You can finish the inner car bodies for six cars in the same evening you would do one and have the glue drying overnight on six or twelve cars instead of just one. Repeating the same steps is quicker when your fingers are still used to the work. Twelve cars is about the limit for even an experienced modeler; try four or six the first time. Attempting too many can make the project more work than enjoyment.

Camino and Northeastern sell the roof, floor and end materials, scribed wood sheet for the sides, roof and ends and strip wood for the underframe, facia strips, door slides and roof walk. CalScale has plastic brake cylinders, and there are dozens of truck bolsters, grab irons and decals to complete the project. Use one or more of the all-wood kits as your guide to sizes, and don't even attempt the project if you haven't already assembled at least one of the all-wood kits. The model railroad magazines publish plans occasionally; there are others in the hardback books on specific real railroads, and each of the rolling stock editions of the Newton K. Gregg *Train Shed 'Cyclopedia* paperbacks has plans. You will, in most instances, have to reduce the prototype's dimensions to scale feet and inches, so you will need a scale ruler or one of the PFM HO or O scale vernier calipers.

If you like to work with plastic, I can recommend the line of scribed sheets, plain sheets and strips in styrene from Evergreen. Styrene is a bit easier to cut than the bass wood commonly used for model railroad kits, because you can just scribe a light cut where you want it and break the styrene cleanly along the cut line. The broken edge should be sanded (with number 200-grit sandpaper) or filed smooth, but so should a cut through wood. If you use liquid cement for plastics, the styrene can be glued almost as quickly as you can attach the

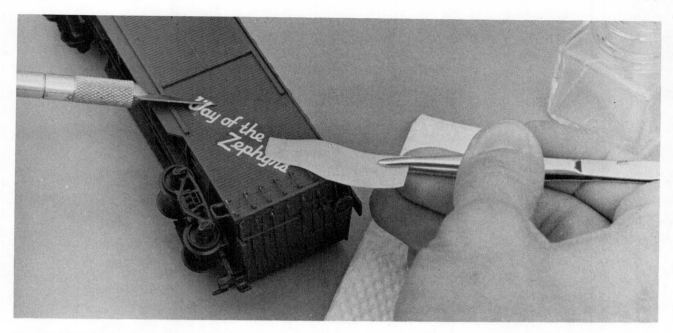

Fig. 4-10 Hold the decal with tweezers to position it over the side of the car, then use the tip of a hobby knife to keep the decal in place while you slide the paper backing from beneath it with tweezers.

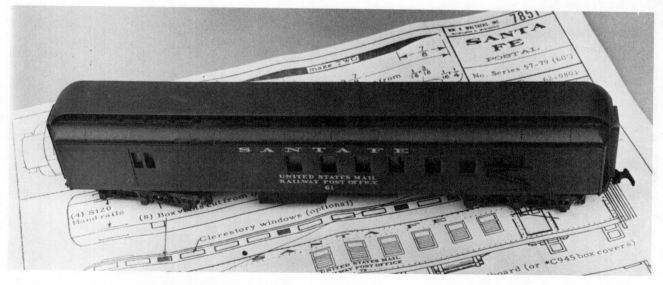

Fig. 4-11 This conversion car utilized Walthers stamped metal car sides with an AHM ready-to-run coach roof and floor cut and shortened to match the car sides.

parts, especially when you are assembling six or more cars at a time.

I would suggest that you use the conventional wood inner floor, ends and roof like the all-wood car kits with the plastic for the outer surfaces, underframe, facia and the roof walk. The grain and scribe lines in wood are actu-

ally a bit oversize for HO or N scales, so the Evergreen plastic looks more realistic than wood after it is painted. Wood is, in my opinion, still the best material for O scale models where the wood grain is more obvious on the finished car. You might want to use wood for the roof walks of an all-plastic car body just to

Fig. 4-12   This AHM ready-to-run baggage car was converted to a Harriman-style car by splicing together two MDC Harriman roof sections and installing a metal Walthers baggage door.

Fig. 4-13   Paul Harris spliced two ConCor N scale baggage-car bodies together to make this baggage car with equal-size doors.

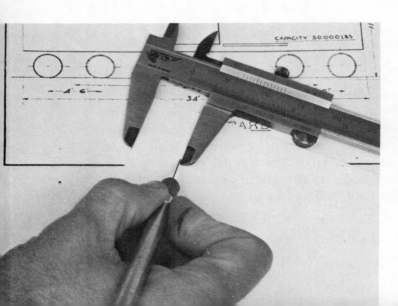

Fig. 4-14   Evergreen and other brands of sheet styrene are easy to work with when scratch-building cars. Use a PFM caliper or a scale ruler with plans of the proto- type to mark off the sizes. Mark the lines with a pencil, then make a single cut with a hobby knife.

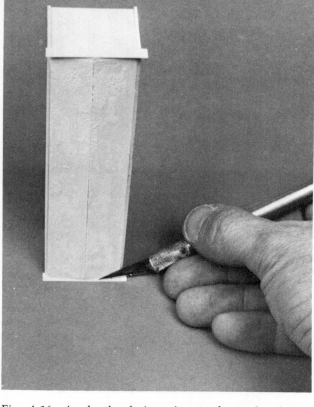

Fig. 4-15 It is not necessary to cut all the way through the sheet styrene with the hobby knife. A cut .005-inch deep is enough for sheets up to .040-inch thick. Hold the cut directly over a sharp table edge and simply break the pieces apart along the cut line.

Fig. 4-16 Apply the facia strips to the ends of the roof just before the roof sheathing is installed so you can trim the thin plastic to match the angle of the roof.

show the rough grain that often was apparent on the wooden roof walks of full-size cars. Use .010-inch-thick plastic to assemble models of steel-sheathed cars by punching or embossing imitation rivet heads on the backside of the plastic sheet. Northwest Short Line

makes a small punch and die set and table for modelers that is perfect for forming rivets, because the table can be moved by turning a micrometerlike knob to obtain even rivet spacing. The inner walls can be constructed just like those in the all-wood kits.

Fig. 4-17 The all-plastic car is constructed in the same manner as a LaBelle, Scotia, Central Valley or Camino all-wood car (top), but the components are all Evergreen-brand plastic strips and sheet stock.

Scale Performance

The realistic operation of miniature trains has become almost as important as the appearance of the models. The development of reliable Kadee automatic couplers and solid-state speed controls has made switching and smooth starts and stops the goal of most model railroaders. Now a modeler will pay as much attention to the performance as to the looks of a prospective addition to his or her locomotive roster. There are enough choices of both steam and diesel locomotives, especially in HO scale, for the discerning modeler to make that kind of choice. The toy train locomotives still have a top speed equal to about twice that of the prototype, and they still won't operate at much less than a scale 10 miles an hour. That type of drag racing or slingshot performance can be avoided by buying brands intended for the hobbyist or by adding one of the better-performing locomotive chassis to a desirable superstructure in place of the toylike stock chassis.

There has been much publicity over the years about the absolute top speed of real trains like the Turbo and Metroliner runs.

Much less attention is paid to how fast is normal for a freight train (unless you happen to be caught by one at a grade crossing when you're late for an appointment). Some of the master model railroaders became interested in rebuilding the too-fast steam and diesel locomotives so they would perform at speeds more like the prototypes. Diesel engines geared for main-line operation—some have lower gear ratios for switching and peddler freight operations—can operate up to 100 miles an hour on those stretches of real railroad track that are maintained well enough to keep a train on the rails at those speeds. The "super" power locomotives that were built near the end of steam's reign, like the 4-8-4s, were sometimes designed for 100 mph speeds, and even some of the Americans, Atlantics and Praries (2-6-2s) of the turn of the century and the twenties could run along at 90 mph. A typical HO scale ready-to-run diesel or steam locomotive will run between 100 and 177 miles an hour!

These speeds, by the way, are based on the mile part of miles per hour being reduced by 1/87 for an HO scale mph figure; the hour remains the same. An N scale locomotive should have an even slower speed because its mile is reduced to 1/160 that of the real thing; O scale locomotives are slightly faster thanks to their 1/48 reduction in the length of the mile. There are no changes in the length of a mile for narrow-gauge equipment, of course; an HOn2, HOn30" or HOn3 locomotive would still have to travel 1/87 of a real mile.

If HO model railroads were 1/87 the size of the real ones in every respect, the discussion could end right here. A model railroad, even a giagantic club layout like the Highland Pacific, is a scale replica of the real thing in every respect except the actual length of the trackage. There just isn't space for a model railroad with 50-mile lengths of track. The result is that our trains travel from one town to the next, or even from one end of the freight yard to the other, far too quickly. If that HO scale 100-mile-an-hour diesel would stay on the track through all the curves and switches at that speed, it would travel over that barn-size Highland Pacific layout in

Fig. 5-1 Four types of flywheels including (left) F.E.D.'s "drifter" boxcar chassis with flywheel and (l to r) Athearn's SW-1500 (SW-7), Atlas's SD-24, Proto Power West's SW-500 (SW-7) and their GP-9.

about five minutes; it would cover most home layouts in a matter of seconds. Model locomotives should, then, run much slower than their prototypes just to help us complete the realistic effects we strive for in every other aspect of the hobby.

A model railroad is built for fun; a real railroad is built for profit and efficiency. The real railroads might want those 100 mph capabilities to rush a trainload of containers from the seaports to the midwest. In a few rare instances—too few for the profitability of the lines—the real railroads have trackwork good enough to run fast trains. In the reality, however, even the real trains operate at high speeds over only about 5 percent of their routes. For one thing, there are only a very few hotshot freights on any real railroads, and the express passenger trains disappeared

after World War II. If you were to operate one train out of a hundred at even 60 scale miles an hour, you'd be close enough to the actual performance of the real railroads.

I don't want to confuse you with average speeds or the timetable operations of the real railroads; those figures include stop, start and waiting. For now, it's the traveling pace of the motive power and how long it takes for it to accelerate and decelerate to that speed that's important. Most main lines are posted for 50 miles an hour for freights; that same stretch used to be posted 60 for passenger trains. The actual speeds are at least 10 miles an hour below that. All this discussion has been background information to help you understand why 40 scale miles an hour is fast for a model train even when operated on a club layout!

The real railroads are concerned with getting goods from one point to another thousands of miles away as inexpensively as possible. Those few hotshot TrailerTrain (TOFC and COFC) trains, fruit express trains and some of the unit coal trains are the few exceptions. That's why a railroad in financial trouble, as the Rock Island was in the seventies, or the Penn Central, could survive with most of its main-line trackage in such poor repair that it was posted for a maximum of 10 to 20 miles an hour. The steam-powered (and diesel too) coal drags over the Appalachians and the standard and narrow-gauge runs through the Colorado Rockies moved at between five and 10 miles an hour! Most of the articulated locomotives were limited to about a 35-mile-an-hour top speed regardless of conditions.

A model locomotive has some problems with physics that do not apply to a real locomotive. The real ones have no trouble whatsoever moving through a yard at a walking pace. With all that weight, smooth stops and slow starts are normal. One of the problems with a model locomotive is that we can scale down just about everything but gravity, so that the weight of our models is never quite enough. We have problems with oxidation of the wheels and rails that make a smooth flow of electricity to the motor unpredictable.

The electrical power for our models presents yet another problem in that none of the motors that will fit inside an HO scale locomotive have an operating speed range that will allow *both* 3-miles-an-hour switching (or the smooth starts and stops that begin

Fig. 5-2 A locomotive and car repair cradle, made from three 1-foot lengths of 1" x 2" wood and a scrap of cloth, will help to minimize damage to your equipment. Use a pipe cleaner dipped in solvent to clean grease and dirt from between the drivers and frame.

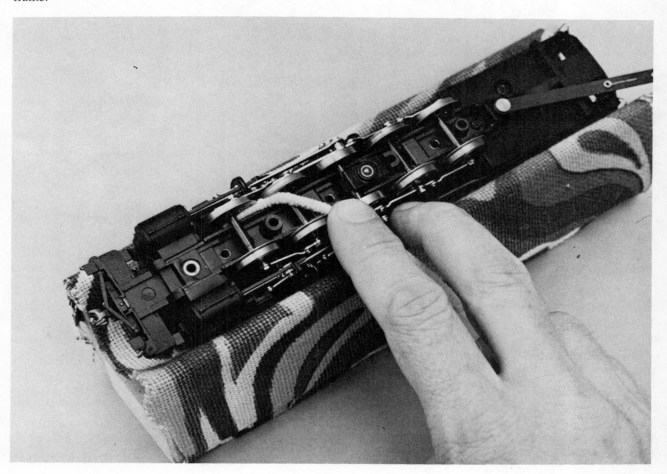

Scenes like this are what model railroading is all about. Felix Medak's repainted and detailed N scale diesel is rounding the high trestle on the East Valley Model Railroad Club's layout.

Van S. Facko added extra details, like the typical Southern Pacific snow plows, to this trio of Athearn diesels rounding a curve on the Highland Park Society of Model Engineers layout.

Industrial clutter is one element of real railroading that adds realism to any model layout. Most of these structures are altered plastic kits with extra paint, detailing and a touch of weathering.

Marshall Nelson's fine HO scale layout has its own spare room that doubles as an attached den. The terrain and the trains are typical of the southwest.

The Highland Park Society of Model Engineers HO scale layout has the 36-inch minimum-radius curves needed for realistic operation of full-length streamliners.

The water is epoxy casting resin with ground and sifted granite for the rocks and dirt.
This is all but a few inches (to the right) of Frank Barone's On3 module.

An example of the differences in size and track gauge of narrow and standard-gauge equipment on Marshall Nelson's layout. The locomotives are brass imports.

Most of the structures on Marshall Nelson's layout are kits with new paint and altered details to give them a unique appearance.

Mark Henley added a second story to a Revell HO scale freight house to completely alter its appearance and mounted it on a foot-square base with a section of hand-laid track.

A diorama need only be an inch or two larger than the structure it features. Denis Dunning assembled this Fine Scale feed mill.

The Colorado Midland's Colorado City yard as it was in 1910. Forrest Van Schwartz, Don Meeker and Daryl Ryder built this 4 x 6-foot diorama in HO scale to display Model Masterpieces' roundhouse. Model Masterpieces Ltd. photo by Donald Meeker.

A Locomotive Company standard-gauge engine arrives at Mark Henley's scratch-built station just in time to pick up the passengers from Wayne Lyndon's C-16 consolidation on the narrow-gauge high line.

Lonnie Shay is one of the finest scenery artists in the world. All of the rocks on his HOn3 layout are cast from plaster in latex rubber molds.

Two by four feet is plenty, even in 0 scale, for a modular layout like Frank Barone's. All of the structures are scratch-built. The locomotives and cars are detailed commercial products by Dennis Weaver.

Wayne Lyndon painted and decaled this HO scale engine to match the brand-new appearance of many steam locomotives in the 1910–1940 era.

The rugged Rockies looked just like this when the narrow gauge entered them in the 1800s to help haul out the gold and silver.

A portion of a Revell engine house and an AHM store were combined to create this realistic trolley barn and street diorama. Scott Alexander and Mark Henley are responsible for this HO scale scene.

Jeff Abbott's GP-9 diesels growl their way up the grade through the scenery that Paul Harris and Larry Larson built on the East Valley Model Railroad Club's layout.

The distant mountains are an HO West brand backdrop on Lonnie Shay's layout. He fits each of his locomotives with lower gearing and a precision motor so they run just as realistically as they look.

and end with that kind of minimum speed) and 70 miles an hour or more top speeds. Model Die Casting (MDC) pioneered ultralow gearing in HO scale locomotive kits. The MDC kits and those from Bowser, Proto Power West, Kemtron, Penn Line and The Locomotive Company will operate at about 2 scale miles an hour if the mechanisms are broken in properly and lubricated with La-Belle number 106 grease rather than oil. Most of the other kits and ready-built locomotives will only operate at 5 to 10 scale miles an hour. The imported brass locomotives offer performance characteristics that are completely unrelated to their price; some have as a high a starting and top speed as the toy trains, and others will crawl to those 2 scale mph speeds. Be prepared to do some work on most of the ready-to-run locomotives, whether they're plastic or brass.

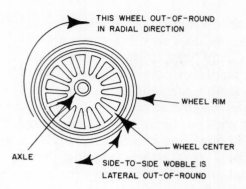

Fig. 5-3 An exaggerated view of two types of wheel or driver misalignment.

SLOW SPEED PERFORMANCE

There are about four different ways to obtain slow and smooth performance from a model locomotive. You can achieve some astonishing results by disassembling the chassis and checking each wheel or driver, each gear, and each portion of the drive rods (the main rods and side rods) and valve gear (the smaller rods on modern steamers) on steam locomotives. Use crocus cloth (the finest grade of emery paper—hardware stores sell it) to smooth rough axles and the sides of frames. Polish the axle bearings with the smooth end of the nearest size drill bit. Use a jewelers' round (needle) file to enlarge the holes in steam locomotive drive rods so there is no bind. The HO scale NMRA standard's gauge has slots and tabs that should be used to check the wheel spacing on every locomotive and car you have. If the wheels are spaced improperly, they can usually be moved with some strong finger pressure—do not twist any steam locomotive drivers on their axles or you'll change the angle of the crank pins (the "quartering" of the drivers). Be sure that the locomotive runs as freely with

the superstructure in place as it does as a bare chassis. Pay particular attention to the mesh between the gears so there is just a perceptible amount of free movement at the gear teeth, but not so much as to allow the teeth to strip and not so little that the gears will bind. You may even need to install some phosphor bronze pickup shoes to rub the rails beneath the cylinders of a steam locomotive and the tender trucks or diesel trucks. GH Products makes several styles, or you can assemble your own from spring brass and nickel silver. The sliding pickup will break through dust and oxidation where a rolling wheel or driver will not.

The type of throttle you use can also affect the slow speed performance of your model locomotives. The power packs sold in most train sets have rheostats that are wound with too few wires to give a smooth starting speed control. I'd recommend the inexpensive MRC Cab 55 walk-around throttle control as the least expensive way to add a good slow-speed control to your power pack; it will also let you sample the advantages of the walk-around control in Chapter VIII. The transistorized throttles and speed controls are the best answer; they range in price from about $40 to $150, and you usually get what you pay for. I do not recommend the power packs or throttles with pulse power switches or circuitry because they introduce spikes of power into the circuit, which can overheat some of the totally enclosed can motors. Don't overlook dirty or crooked or out-of-gauge trackwork as a cause for erratic locomotive performance and lack of slow speed control either.

The third way to improve the slow speed performance of your locomotives is to lower the overall gear ratio. This type of work is definitely for the advanced modeler who is familiar with model mechanics in general. Northwest Short Line makes many styles of gears including kits for some specific models. The installation of lower gearing usually demands that the wheels or drivers be removed so the axle gear can be replaced; the correct reassembly and alignment (quartering of steam locomotive drivers) is tricky at best. An alternative solution is to replace the complete chassis. Hobbytown and Proto Power West make fine-running HO scale diesel chassis for Athearn superstructures, and they can be adapted to fit most other brands including the brass imports. The Bowser, Penn Line and Locomotive Company chassis are available as separate kits. They can be adapted to most brass locomotives as well.

The fourth alternative method of improving locomotive performance is almost as complex as changing the gearing; change the motor by fitting one of the can-style motors from Northwest Short Line and Westside. These motors have a lower top speed and a lower starting speed that can have almost the same effect as a change to a lower gear ratio. Again, however, the concept of changing a motor demands a knowledge of modeling that few of us possess. The Proto Power West and Locomotive Company chassis have can motors, or you can contact one of the shops like Whistle Stop (Pasadena) or The Little Depot, which specialize in both gear and can motor installations in HO, HOn3 and N scale locomotives. Realistic performance is going to run at least $40 and maybe as much as $150, whether you buy a complete chassis or have a custom motor/gear change fitted to your locomotive. If you want to run your locomotives as well as look at them, it's the best investment you can make. If you want multiple-unit diesels, you can always make just one unit per "lash-up" the superperformer and the rest dummies.

Fig. 5-4 There is no shortcut to smooth locomotive performance. If there is a bind in the chassis, strip it down until only one of the side rods is attached and the motor is out to check for free-rolling. Next try it with the opposite side rod in place.

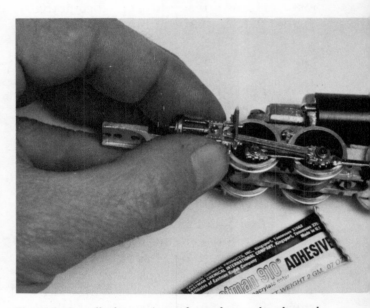

Fig. 5-5 Install the main rods and crossheads and guides to check first the right and then the left set for bind-free operation. The nonworking parts can be attached with one of the cyanoacrylate cements.

FLYWHEELS

The flywheel was one of the first methods that modelers discovered in their quest for smoother locomotive performance. The momentum feature of most transistorized throttles and power packs has the same effect on the locomotive's speed as a flywheel by doing just what you'd expect, maintaining momentum for smoother starts and slower stops. Most of the newest ready-to-run diesels in both HO and N scale are now being fitted with flywheels at the factory. The flywheel is one of those practical applications of a physics principle; the flywheel's mass serves to store some of the motor's energy. The motor has to work against the flywheel to get turning, and once it's going, the flywheel will just coast along with it so there's no meaningful loss of efficiency. When the motor is slowed, the flywheel keeps on rotating, or "wants" to, because it has that stored energy in its rotational force and mass. The net result is that the model locomotive will have somewhat smoother starts and smoother stops, and even more important, it will often coast over some of the spots where a conventional chassis might stall. Hobbytown was one of the first to offer a flywheel, in the fifties, and they're now standard on Athearn, Atlas and Proto Power West products. The flywheel is no substitute for proper gearing, a good motor and clean track and wheels, but it can contribute marginally to locomotive performance.

ROLLING STOCK

You can begin to understand that there is a lot more to smooth and controllable model train performance than just turning a knob. The trackwork, power supply, throttle, gearing, locomotive weight and motor all play an important part. The weight and rolling qualities of the individual cars are almost as important as the other factors in model railroading. Every one of your freight and passenger cars should have the same rolling friction. If one or two cars have more friction than the others, those cars can put a bind in the train's operations that can cause derailments. Cars that roll too freely, as compared to the rest of your equipment, can cause the same type of problem because the locomotive will pull "through" them and derail them while it's

Fig. 5-6 One of the most frequent trouble spots, on a steam locomotive chassis, is the clearance between the crossheads and the main rod-attaching screws. You may have to file the ends of the main rod screws to obtain adequate clearance.

trying to get the other cars rolling. The only solution here is to set up an inclined test track and roll each car down it. Adjust the angle so the best-rolling cars will just start moving on their own. The cars with more friction will have to be fiddled with to determine if they can be loosened up; clean the pointed tips of the axles and the bearings in the truck side frames, remove any gum from the wheels, check the gauge of the wheels, and look for any burrs or other reasons why the wheels won't spin freely. In some cases you may have to purchase new wheel sets or complete new trucks to get all of the cars rolling the same way.

The weight of the rolling stock has an effect very similar to trucks with too much friction. The NMRA has conducted tests on TT, HO and S scale railroads and determined that the car length can also affect its weight. The NMRA "Recommended Practices" study number RP20.1 suggests that your shortest cars should weigh 1 ounce in HO scale (¾ ounce in TT and 2 ounces in S scales), and that ½ ounce should be added for each additional ounce of car weight (add ⅜ ounce for TT and ½ ounce for S scales). If you are modeling a modern railroad, then your shortest car might be a 40-foot boxcar or caboose; if you're modeling the twenties or earlier, you might well have some 28-foot tank cars or cabooses that are even shorter. Lead fishing sinkers can be cemented inside the cars, or you can use thin strips of typesetter's lead. The weight might have to be built into flat cars, gondolas and hoppers by trimming away some of the underframe braces on the bottom of the car to fit blocks or thin strips of lead. Notice that the TT scale cars would be about the same size as HOn30″ or HOn2 equipment and only slightly smaller than HOn3 rolling stock, so you can use those standards to improve the performance of your narrow-gauge rolling stock as well. The S scale standards would be very close to correct for On2 and On3 equipment.

The mounting of the trucks and couplers on freight and passenger cars can also cause or cure problems. Couplers mounted on the trucks allow long cars and locomotives to negotiate very small-radius curves, but they don't look much like the prototype. If your cars are too long for your layout's curves, the layout's realism is going to suffer with or without the strange coupler locations and the resulting lack of end sill detail. The truck-mounted couplers work pretty well when a train is being pulled, but they can be a frequent cause of derailments when the train is being pushed or backed. If you must have long cars and tight curves, then think seriously about building your layout with smaller-scale equipment so the curves are not so tight in proportion to the size of the rolling stock. An 18-inch radius curve is just too tight

for anything but Gay Nineties or earlier equipment in HO scale or for a logging layout, but 18 inches is just enough for even 80-foot cars in N scale, and it's fine for the short HOn3 or HOn2 or HOn30″ narrow-gauge cars and locomotives.

The mounting of the trucks to the bolsters can be another source of trouble. If the bolsters are tight enough so the cars won't wobble, then the trucks can't lean to compensate for slight track irregularities, and the cars will derail. The solution is to provide a three-point suspension system for each of your cars by making the truck pivot as tight as possible on one end of the car and very loose on the other. The tight bolster will prevent lean by keeping the weight on at least two of the truck's wheels on its end of the car, and the loose bolster will give a single pivot point so that truck will be able to lean a bit to follow the track more precisely. If your trucks are attached with screws, it's a simple matter of tightening or loosening the screw. If you use the press-in or snap-in type of bolster mounts found on most all-plastic cars, then you may have to enlarge the hole slightly and/or fill the hole with five-minute epoxy to get the trucks adjusted properly. This tight/loose system will also help to stop that toylike car sway that is so common on model railroads. Some of the sway and derailment problems that affect diesel locomotives can be corrected by filing and shimming the diesel truck pivots, so one truck can only pivot while the one on the opposite end can both privot and rock from side to side.

Bench Work, Track Work and Wiring

Model railroaders, as a group, are "make-do" people. If they find something they want, they'll find a way to get it, even if that means improvising or using unconventional means. This may be because a vivid imagination is what draws most people to this hobby in the first place. Finding space for a model railroad is one problem area in which innovation is the rule. Almost everyone in the hobby would like to have an empty barn—heated and air conditioned, of course—for his or her layout. Only a fraction of a percent of us ever get that much room, and even if we do, it is probably as part of the club in our area.

The availability of spare space is shrinking in this country as housing costs increase, but in spite of that, there are more model railroaders than ever before. Some of us have been lured into the hobby by the space-saving promises of N scale or Z scale, but even that only reduces the space we'd like to half a barn. One of the answers to the space problem has been to build a complete model railroad in pieces just big enough to fit on a bookshelf. The pieces assemble later into that future dream layout, or they can be transported to the garage or some club gathering to be joined by others who have similar-sized pieces. The concepts I'm referring to fall under the general categories of dioramas, shelf or bookshelf layouts and modules.

DIORAMAS

A diorama is the smallest practical size for even a piece of a model railroad. In fact, I've seen a diorama with an HO scale hand car, a hand car house and a very short length of track which was only 4 inches square and as realistic as anything you'd see in a contest. I've also seen dioramas of sawmills and steel mills that were the size of a Ping-Pong table and still not close to being complete models of those operations. The basic thinking behind a diorama is to build a structure or a small scene that is complete unto itself, with trackage and complete scenery. Most such dioramas will eventually find their way onto the builder's permanent layout. Many of the

Modular Model Railroading

structures on Irv Schultz's layout in Volume I were constructed as dioramas, entered in national NMRA contests and—in some cases after winning blue ribbons—plopped into prefitted holes on his layout. Marshall Nelson interchanges a dozen different dioramas between his home layout (in Chapter II) and his HO scale module in this chapter. A diorama is certainly not just exercise but an investment of time and experience in your next layout, and if you like, it can be a part of any layout you ever build.

Mark Henley is a diorama specialist; two examples of his work are on page 66. He is a writer and photographer by avocation who has had dozens of articles published in national magazines like *Railroad Modeler*. Many of his dioramas, including those shown here, are sold by The Whistle Stop hobby shop in Pasadena, California. There are many other shops that offer dioramas for sale; it's one way for those who would rather build locomotives or cars to have a superbly realistic place to display them. The "pure" armchair model railroader might find this one

Fig. 6-1 Mark Henley scratch-built this two-level station diorama with an A.I.M. cast plaster retaining wall to separate the track levels.

Fig. 6-2 Mark Henley uses a combination of ground foam, Boyd-brand "grass" flocking, lichen and cattail "weeds" to create his realistic ground coverings.

Fig. 6-3 An assortment of dioramas or foot-square (plus) model railroads that would fit nicely on a single bookshelf and still leave room for some model and real railroad books.

way to lend a third dimension to his or her two-dimensional enjoyment of the hobby. Most of us, obviously, are in the hobby to build models like dioramas for ourselves.

Dioramas are more interesting if there is at least an inch of terrain on all sides of any structure. If you have a track or two on the diorama, however, the edge of the diorama should be only about ⅛ inch away from the track so you will be able to insert the diorama in your layout without cutting it. The best way around the problem is to add a 1-inch-wide strip of ½-inch Homosote between the track and the edge of the diorama. Attach both the diorama's ½-inch Homosote and the

strip to a piece of ½-inch plywood or another piece of Homosote with wood screws, so that forward edge can be easily broken when the time comes to install the diorama on your future layout. All the structure, weathering and scenery suggestions in this book and in Volume I can be applied to the diorama as readily as they can to a complete model railroad.

THE MODULE

The aerospace industry's terminology has changed what once were simply portable model railroads into what are now called

Fig. 6-4   Gordon Johnson scratch-built this 6 x 18-inch diorama of a Canadian Pacific steam locomotive sandhouse. Like all such scenes, it can decorate your bookshelf until your dream layout is complete enough to accept the scene.

modules. Model railroaders who were officers in any one of the armed forces have been building portable layouts for almost 50 years. The concept has taken on new meaning in the seventies, thanks to the enterprise of the people who founded NTRAK. The NTRAK club publishes an inexpensive design manual that stipulates the size of a member module, its wiring, track locations and other factors that must be standardized for that NTRAK module to fit any other NTRAK module. The system works well enough so that there are now over 200 NTRAK modules throughout the world, and any one will connect to any other. Some gigantic layouts result when there is an NTRAK gathering at, for example, one of the NMRA national conventions. There's an NTRAK module in this chapter; there were several others in Volume I.

The NTRAK *Manual* is as complete a description of the specifics of the system as you could want. If you are planning on building a portable layout of any kind, whether to interchange with NTRAK (in N scale only), to interchange with one of the HO scale groups, On3 clubs or just to interchange with itself so you have a layout that can move whenever you do, then buy that NTRAK manual and duplicate the wiring and construction details as closely as you can. The NTRAK *Manual* is $1 from Jim Fitzgerald, 2424 Alturas Road, Atascadero, California 93422. A subscription to the *NTRAK Newsletter*, a bimonthly publication of N scale ideas and a calendar and report on NTRAK gatherings, is another $3 per year.

There is another group of N scale modular model railroaders with international membership and with module design specifications that allow more freedom of track locations at the expense of some degree of interchangeability. The INTERAIL Modular

Fig. 6-5 The late John Allen was one of the model railroaders who helped develop the switching layout that is used for contests at many National Model Railroad Association conventions. With a few structures, it would make a fine operating bookshelf layout.

Railway System Manual is $5 from IN-TERAIL, Box 99437, San Francisco, California 94109. The INTERAIL module designs include some that will interface (join) with the NTRAK modules as well as hexes and other rectangular shapes besides NTRAK's 2 x 4 or 2 x 6-foot standards. A subscription to the INTERAIL magazine *Interchange* is $1 for each issue. INTERAIL is one of the few groups that promotes modeling of British, European and other foreign prototypes as well as models of American equipment. Their publications will be of primary interest to those in N scale.

The HO scale modeling fraternity has not taken to the modular concept as rapidly or as enthusiastically as N scale modelers have. There are several clubs that work more or less to NTRAK standards, but so far no truly national group. Part of the reason for this may well be that N scale is at its best when used to recreate scenes with long trains of relatively modern equipment. The triple-track mainline design of NTRAK's modules and gatherings of dozens of such modules have allowed operations of trains with 300 or more cars. You can do that in HO scale, but if you wanted to, there are clubs in every major city (ask at the hobby shops to find them) with layouts large enough for that kind of operation. There are fewer N scale clubs because that scale is newer than HO, and perhaps because the need for long-train operation can be filled by the more up-to-date club concept of NTRAK modules.

There are four HO modular layout clubs that you might want to contact and one that works in O and On3 scales:

The Southern California Modular Railroad
Club (HO scale)
    % Campbell Scale Models
    P.O. Box 121
    Tustin, CA 92680

Tom Maladecki
    HOTrack
    4657 Brougham Drive
    Rockford, IL 61111

Bob Henderson
    HOTRAK
    6426 No. 76th St.
    Milwaukee, WI 53233

George Bates
    Southern California Module Club
        (HO scale)
    9701 Rhea Ave.
    Northridge, CA 91324

Fig. 6-6 Michael Douglas Bishop's NTRAK diorama is a flat 2 x 4-foot masterpiece with nothing but finely sifted sawdust, real dirt from Oklahoma's Red River Valley, lichen and ground foam for scenery. The track is hand-spiked Rail Craft rail and ties.

Fig. 6-7 Jim Fitzgerald connects his two 2 x 6-foot NTRAK modules end-to-end with two half-circle end modules and a three-track straight behind the backdrop to make a layout for either home or NTRAK use.

Fig. 6-8 Most of the structures on this HO scale modular layout are the same ones Marshall Nelson uses on his permanent home layout. The structures and their bases fit cutouts on both his portable modules or his permanent layout.

On3 TRACK Modular Railroading
  ℅ The Train Works
  14341 Beach Blvd.
  Westminster, CA 92683

All of these groups are run by hobbyists, so if you expect any reply, enclose a stamped, self-addressed envelope and be prepared to wait until they find the time to answer you. There will likely be a charge for copies of their specifications; that might well be your first question to them. You can use their specifications to assemble your own home layout modules or to form a local club. If you or one of your club's members is vacationing near one of these groups, you might—by prior appointment, of course—be able to connect your module to some of theirs just as the NTRAK members do. Most of these groups at least try to have gatherings of their members' modules at the national or regional NMRA conventions, and that too might be chance for your module to become a part of a club-size layout. Most of the modular clubs try to have their layouts on display at malls and other shop-

ping centers at least once each year, to help promote the hobby in general and to draw more members into their club in particular. Any of these gatherings of modular layouts are fine places for you to see what a layout like this can look like, even if you're not yet ready to add your own module to the layout.

Each of the modules that belong to any of the modular layout groups is designed primarily to be a place where its builder can operate trains at home. None of the designs can really be operated as anything more than a switching site by itself. You can do what Jim Fitzgerald (one of the NTRAK founders) does and couple one or two modules, two end loops and some straight track to make an oval layout for true train operations at home. You'll need at least 2½ x 6 feet of space for an NTRAK layout like that and about 5 x 9 feet for an HO layout. You might want to consider a layout that gives you a bit more freedom of design if you have that much space available for a home layout, or take a close look at the INTERAIL modules.

Fig. 6-9 The fence and telephone wires on Mike Bishop's NTRAK module are cotton threads sprayed with Testor's Dullcote to kill the shine and prevent any fuzz. Superb realism from details that are too obvious for most modelers to remember to build.

THE SWITCHING LAYOUT

Moving freight or passenger cars in and out of sidings without touching them by hand is one of the more interesting types of operation for a model railroad. That is also the only kind of operation you're going to get on one of these bookshelf-size modular model railroads. It's important that you be aware of that fact when you design your modular layout's trackwork, so you can include the necessary runaround track (see Chapter X) and enough spur tracks and industries to make it interesting. Most of the modular groups insist that the track (in the case of On3) or tracks (three of them for NTRAK) along the front of the layout be placed to match the ends of all other modules. For home operation, however, those tracks can be operated as stub-end sidings. You are free to place tracks just about anywhere else in the module and still have a layout to meet the specifications of any of the modular groups.

One of the most successful switching layouts for a shelf appeared years before NTRAK or any of the other modules. One of the greatest model railroaders of all time, the late John Allen, created his Timesaver switch-ing layout on a 76-inch length of 1 x 12-inch soft pine, which is actually only about ¾ x 10½ inches. The layout was used for switch-ing contests at NMRA conventions, where the participants competed against the clock to complete a specific series of movements. The speed control was set so the switching loco-motive ran about 7 scale miles per hour and so there was no need to move a throttle; the only controls were for the track switches and a reversing switch with a center "off" position to control the locomotive. The number of cars was usually about five, and the rules were written to make every participant switch the cars from one set of sidings to another to sim-ulate the arrival of loaded cars to replace un-loaded ones on some of the sidings. The two shortest stub-end sidings were designed to accommodate just two cars each, although the Timesaver in the photograph has been lengthened a bit so that map pins limit the useful lengths of some of the sidings. The operation of the layout is one of the most useful methods of learning how to operate a switch engine on a model railroad. It helps the operator to understand some of the sequences that can help to save time when maneuvering cars.

Fig. 6-10 Three trestles (one burned to the ground) highlight Frank Barone's On3 module. There's room enough on a 2 x 4-foot module for even O scale equipment like Dennis Weaver's PFM Rio Grande 4-6-0 and his rolling stock.

Fig. 6-11 The trees, switch stands and another half-inch of epoxy resin water will make Frank Barone's On3 modular layout even more realistic. The trees and structures are removable to make transporting the module easier.

The timesaver layout would be far more interesting if expanded to a 2-foot width to leave space for some scale-model industrial buildings along the back. Add a station and perhaps one of the HO West painted backdrops, and you'll have a complete town ready to plop into that permanent layout when you find the space for it. The structures could even include a station and some locomotive servic-ing facilities without interfering at all with the switching value of the layout. This design has been built in HO scale and, with the proportions reduced, in HOn3 and N scale. Just running trains back and forth is bound to become boring; switching cars in and out of sidings with imagined loads or empties is real railroading action that will keep you interested for years.

Switches are one of the most disappointing things in the hobby. You can get over the shock of seeing a streamliner with 80-foot HO scale cars lurching around an 18-inch radius turn, and you can live with six-car trains where you thought you could run 40 cars. The track switches that are compatible with the snap-together track sections somehow seem to only resemble the switches on real railroads. One of the appeals of scale model railroading is that the models look and act very much like the real thing. Those plastic-tied switches don't do either job very well. If they looked that bad and worked, then they could be forgiven, but most of them are constant sources of derailments and the one place where a locomotive is almost guaranteed to stall. There are two approaches to the problem of the poor switch; try to fix it, or spend the time and effort to build your own from kits or from just raw rail.

Switch Work

THE SNAP-SWITCHES

The switches that have plastic ties are generally designed for the toy train market either here or in Europe or Japan. Trackwork is one area of railroad design in which there are not all that many visual differences between countries except for Britain's "bullhead" rail and supports. You can identify the toy switches in an instant by looking at their frogs—the place where the rails cross in the center of the switch; if the frog is plastic rather than brass, steel or nickel silver like the rest of the switch, then you have a toy. The HO scale switches sold by Lambert, the N scale switches sold by ConCor and some of the newest switches in HO scale from Atlas are not toys, and some of the switches with gentle angles from the N scale makers like Rapido and Peco are not in the toy category either.

The toy makers use plastic frogs because that provides a point of total electrical insulation that makes the switch less expensive to make and much easier for the young railroader to play with. You will need to study the flow of electricity through a model railroad switch to understand why the plastic frog is helpful. If electrical current is fed into the switch from the direction of the frog or siding toward the switch points, there is no way, with a plastic frog, that that current can cause a short circuit. If the current reaches the switch points through an all-metal frog, there's a fifty-fifty chance (depending on which way the points face) it will cause a short circuit. The plastic frog eliminates that potential short circuit.

Both the siding and the main-line sides of the switch are "live" with most of these designs, so a train can approach the switch without stalling, regardless of which way the switch is thrown. This can be a situation in which a model railroader might have to install an on-off switch to keep the siding from receiving power, but it's seldom a problem with toy layouts. When the switch frog is all-metal, the electrical current will only flow down the path that the switch points are aligned for. There must be some kind of an electrical gap and an additional wire jumper around the switch if power reaches it from the

Fig. 7-1 The random spacing, colors and textures of individual wood ties are realistic enough to make this method of track laying worth the extra effort. Frank Barone cuts and solders rails to scratch-build his own switches. Note the abandoned ties and burned-out bridge.

frog end (see Volume I for the correct wiring in this situation). That occasional need for one gap in the rails and some jumper wires is a small price to pay for the even flow of electricity through the entire length of the switch—there is no plastic frog to allow locomotives to stall for lack of electrical pickup.

I don't like to suggest that some product you may already have purchased is not what you should have, but I must; if any of your track has brass rails then you're going to have problems as long as you use it. Nickel silver flex track and switches are available in both N and HO scale. The nickel silver will oxidize as quickly as brass, but the oxidation on nickel silver is electrically conductive and that on brass is not. In other words, when your brass rail gets even slightly oxidized, it will cause your locomotives to stall. Coincidentally, most of the toy switches are made with brass rail.

Most of the toy switches are also designed with switch angles far too severe for smooth operation or appearance. There is a grace and flow to the rails of a prototype switch that is an example of form following function. Each and every transition from straight to curved

track on a full-size railroad is done gradually with what is called an easement or transition, a gradually increasing radius curve. Switches are examples of this use of easements. When you watch a full-size train move through a freight yard, it seems to flow almost like a river; a model train traveling through those toy switches does so in a series of lurches. The toy switches have very little easement, and their angles are too severe, so the track will align with 18-inch or smaller radius curves (in HO scale).

The angle of a switch is given as a frog number. This number defines the angle between the rails when they cross each other. The angle is figured in units rather than degrees, much as a grade is figured in percentage rather than degrees. If you arbitrarily pick ¼ inch as the unit for measuring the angle of a switch on an HO scale layout, you would have to move four units (⁴/₄ths or 1-inch) from the frog before the two rails would be one unit (¼ inch) apart. Most toy switches are made to replace sections of curved track in the geometric system of plug-in track sections, so you won't find exactly even frog angles. Most of the toy switches have an angle about equal to a number 4. You won't see a switch that sharp on a real railroad in any place but a tight industrial area or in the streets on a trolley line. Most modern mainline switches are a number 12 or larger. In HO scale, that switch would measure about 15 inches from the points to the frog, far too long to be practical on even a club-size layout. A number 8 switch looks almost as good and needs less than 6 inches from its points to its frog in HO scale. A number 5 or 6 switch is a more practical choice for most model railroads.

The switches with all-metal frogs are sold by their frog angle numbers. If you're modeling a narrow-gauge railroad with small locomotives and cars that are 30 scale feet or so long, then you can use a switch as sharp as a number 4; the real narrow-gauge railroads did. For most model railroads, the number 6 should be considered a minimum frog angle, with number 8s where you want that feeling of main-line operations. The major difficulty with a gentle frog angle is that it limits the length of sidings because it takes so much distance for the siding to get far enough away from the main line to clear the cars. That distance will be even greater if you insist on using snap-together switches, because they all have a bit more straight track on the "curved" siding than is necessary. Don't hesitate to use a razor saw to cut the rails leading to the siding or those on the point end of the switch to locate two switches closer together. This cut-to-fit technique will allow you to squeeze a lot more track into a yard or industrial area without the slightest sacrifice in realism—just be sure to make curves on either end of the switch with easements so you don't create your own trolleylike lurching effect.

I would suggest that you build at least one layout or diorama with ready-laid plastic switches to get the general feeling of working with model railroad track. When you're ready for that ultimate layout, however, you might want to lay your own switches using some of the switch kits like those sold by B-K Enterprises and Rail Craft. When you lay nickel silver rails on individual wood ties, you can

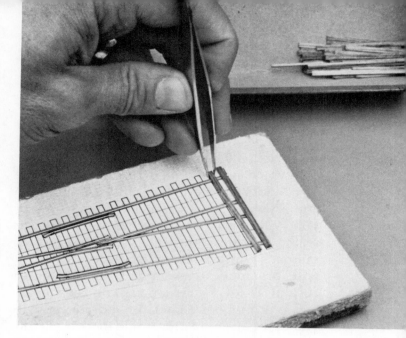

Fig. 7-2 Glue the tie template for the switch right onto the Homosote roadbed with white glue. Precut all of the ties and stain them before gluing them directly onto the template.

Fig. 7-3 Glue fine sandpaper to a wood block to level the surface of the ties in preparation for laying the rails.

use a pencil and a flexible piece of ¼ x 1-inch wood lath to get smooth-flowing easements (transitions from curves to straights) and smoother entrances and exits from switches. Campbell switch ties have tie and switch templates; Timberline sells separate paper templates; or you can draw your own from the information in the NMRA DATA-PAK sheets. Lay the ties in a smooth-flowing pattern and spike the rails to match them.

I would suggest that you consider the switch kits an interim step in learning to file and solder your own switches from pieces of rail. When you build switches to fit, you can really capture the feeling of the actual railroads with curved switches, wye switches with different curves in and out and other custom trackwork. As long as you keep a pattern of a number 6 switch handy to be sure you don't make the frog angle too sharp, you can make any angle you desire at the switch frogs.

HAND-SPIKED SWITCHES

The first step in laying your own switches on wooden ties is to get the ties glued down in the right places. Make some Xerox copies of those switch tie templates and glue them right onto the Homosote roadbed. That will locate the two all-important areas of the switch: the frog and the points. There should be two extra-long ties at the switch points for a simulated (or working) switch stand like those on the prototype. You'll have to cut the switch ties to length even if you use Campbell's HO scale switch ties, so you might save some money by purchasing Northeastern or Camino bass wood strips the same size as the ties you are using.

Use one of the switch tie templates to determine how many ties are needed of each length. Most modelers cut enough ties of each length for a dozen or more switches and place them in a compartmentalized container like an egg carton. Be sure to stain the switch ties the same colors as the regular ties. Glue the ties to the template and sprinkle on enough ballast to fill the area the length of the ties—the rest of the ballast can be glued down later. I'd suggest using white glue to hold the switch ties and their ballast with the more flexible artist's Liquid Matte Medium for the ballast on the edges of the ties. Be sure to

mark the ties where the frog and points are supposed to go before those lines on the template are buried in the ballast. You might want to use a map pin to show where the frog and points are supposed to rest.

Modelers don't agree completely on what is the most important part of the switch to spike in place first—I'd suggest you begin with the switch frog and about an inch or so of the rails on either side of the frog. Use at least two Kadee track gauges (for HO scale) to hold the outside rails (called the stock rails) while you spike them, even if you do have one of the switch kits with soldered-on rail spacers. Spike the straight rail first, and sight down it by eye to be sure it really is straight. Spike the curved stock rail in place last. If you're using one of the switch kits, the guard rails will be soldered to the stock rails. If you're laying your own switch, the bases of the guard rails will have to be notched to clear the spikes on the stock rails and the guard rails then spiked in position. If you are using the Kadee spiker you can drive a few dozen spare spikes into the Homosote and use needlenose pliers to install them around the frog and guard rails so all the spikes will be the same size. Be sure the tie bar between the points can slide freely (remove the ballast from that slot between the two long switch-stand ties) and the switch should be ready for a switch machine and wiring.

SPECIAL SWITCH POINTS

Most of the derailments on a model railroad's switch are caused by the wheel flanges picking at the points of the switch and climbing over the rail. If you're making your own switches, bend and shape the switch points as shown. If you're using one of the switch kits or a ready-laid switch on plastic ties, then file and shape the points to be as close to the drawings as possible. The secret here is to round the tip of each switch point just enough so it can tuck under the rail head (the top of the rail) on the stock rail. Be certain too that the points close tightly against the stock rail.

Fig. 7-4   A B-K Products switch kit is being spiked into place here. The "ties" on tops of the rails are printed circuit-board strips that B-K solders to the rails to hold them until the switch is spiked into position.

Fig. 7-5   Use at least two track gauges, in addition to the soldered-on spacers, to hold the rails while you spike them. The use of the Kadee Spiker is optional.

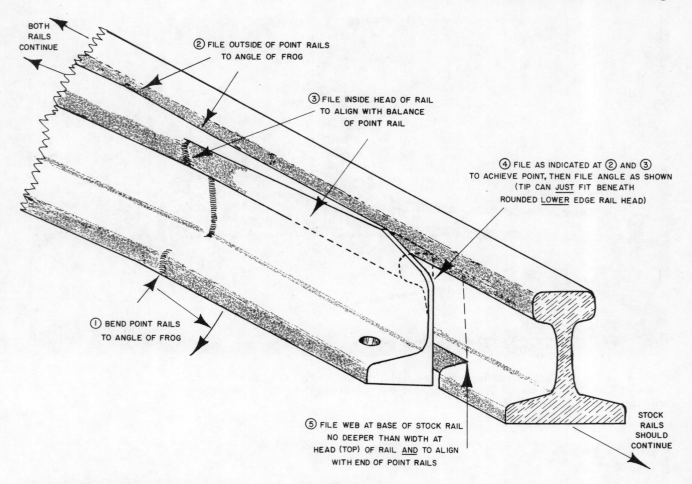

Fig. 7-6 Shaping the ends of switch points to reduce derailments.

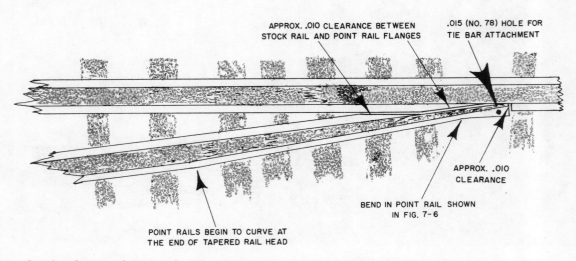

Fig. 7-7 Overhead view of one stock rail and one point rail (angle between the point rail and the stock rail is exaggerated for clarity).

Fig. 7-8   Irv Johnson uses Alexander ground throw switch levers at each switch on his HO/HOn3 layout. The seven levers between the retaining wall and the rear track lead to hidden switches.

Fig. 7-9   Mike Bishop used ready-laid flex track for his N scale main line with Rail Craft ties and rail for this abandoned switch and siding.

The switches on Irv Johnson's HOn3 layout do not have the type of points that now appear on most real railroads. These switches are copies of the stub switches that were used on main-line railroads prior to about 1880 and on the narrow-gauge railroads right up until they laid their last trackage. The rails leading into a stub switch are simply moved to the right or left to align with the curved or straight rails of the switch. The switches on Mr. Johnson's layout are dual-gauge HO and HOn3, which makes the concept confusing. The switch to the far right of the photo is just HOn3, so you can see a conventional application of a stub switch. There was an advantage, on the real railroads, to using the stub switch at high altitudes where freezing conditions were the norm; the switch points would not freeze to the stock rails. The disadvantage of stub switches, for both models and the pro-

totype, is that the points must be aligned perfectly with the diverging rails.

Irv Johnson has devised a clever way of making the at-the-switch ground-throw levers move both the switch and route the electricity down the right path. He uses Alexander's metal ground-throw levers and fits a nickel silver contact to engage the lever of the ground-throw unit. These contacts lead to the diverging routes of the switch so that the right route receives the electrical current. A third wire leads from the ground-throw unit's central base to the frog of the switch to complete the circuit. If the ground-throw lever is not pushed down tightly in its contact, there's no power to the switch rails at all. This system eliminates the need for electric switch machines and the electrical contacts that any all-metal frog switch should have (see Chapter IX).

Some of the fundamental concepts of model railroading have changed over the last few years. There was a time when the dream layout of almost any modeler was one where he or she could sit back and watch a dozen or so trains climbing and twisting through the mountains and across the valleys. The concept is basically a development of the old 4 x 8-foot sheet of plywood with as much snap-together track crammed onto it as there was room. A large percentage of today's model railroad fraternity still believes in that type of model railroading. The goal of having as many trains operating at the same time as possible is especially popular in Europe, and the various brands of ready-to-run European trains and track help make such a layout easier with plug-in relays and other multiple-train control aids. The hobby is heading in a much different direction in America.

More and more American model railroaders are realizing that you can get a maximum amount of realism from any modeling effort by moving your own body in closer to the subject matter. Each modeler has a particular fantasy about trains that he or she wants to fulfill with his or her modeling efforts. For some, the harnessing of tremendous amounts of power in the steam or diesel locomotive is a major attraction in model railroading. Some of us are enthralled by the carefully controlled meets between trains operating right on a timetable's schedule. More and more modelers are drawn to the hobby in trying to recreate the "giant killer" feeling of a narrow-gauge locomotive and its train battling the mountains, or a tiny logging road dragging timber out of the backwoods to the mill. Still others delight at the seemingly eternal success of the railroads in transporting mile-long trains full of the essential goods of life in America. Then there are those that love the history or the industrial archaeology of the railroad industry's glorious past.

There is one common meeting ground that most of the new model railroaders seem to share: an interest in the real railroads that is much greater than it was for a typical model railroader of the fifties. Yesterday's model

Walk-Around Control

railroader could barely tell a Northern from a Mikado, but today's modeler can spot the differences between a GP40 and a GP40-2 at a glance. There is an awakening of interest in how the real railroads are operated and why, and those lessons can be applied to the operation of a model railroad.

The complexity of timetable operation isn't part of every model railroader's goals for his or her own layout, but most of us have some real-life operating concept like the peddler freight or logging short-line antics or passenger terminal action that we want to duplicate on our own layouts. We want our railroads to look like the real thing, we want our locomotives to move like the real thing, and we want our trains to travel through surroundings that give the feeling of the real thing. Some of the smarter folks in the hobby discovered that everything we model looks and feels more like real life when you get closer to the models themselves.

No mortal has ever controlled a real railroad and its trains' paths across the countryside from a control tower. At best, the op-

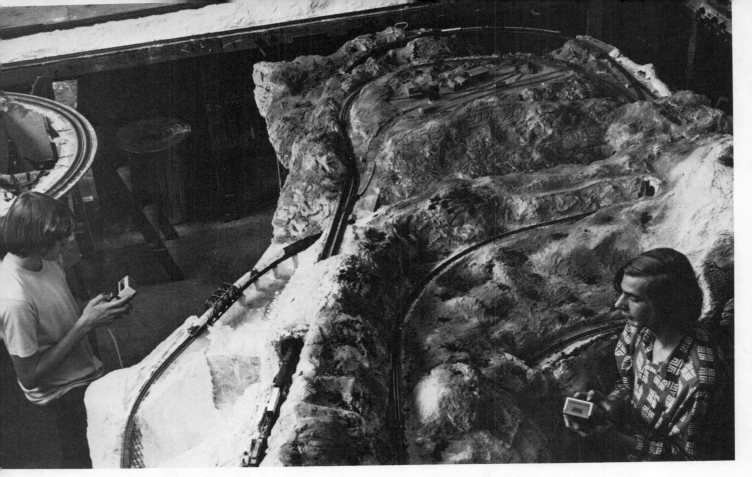

Fig. 8-1   The advantages of shoulder-level trackwork, island-type layout design, a scenic "view break" and walk-around train control are part of the East Valley Lines Club layout.

erators in a control tower see to the end of their freight yard. Most of the dispatchers in those railroad control towers spend their days watching colored lights on control panels that have been duplicated on many model railroads. A real railroad isn't run by a man in a tower watching it. Somewhere along the way to this hobby's maturity, someone realized the truth in that statement when applied to a model railroad. The thrill of watching a train that's twenty feet away respond to your touches at the throttle becomes a game all too quickly. When you're that far removed from your models, it's far too easy to remember that they are indeed models. There is a limit to the most fertile imagination.

The modern concept of model railroading is embodied in the walk-around control system. The idea is that you attach the throttle, reversing switch and, with the more sophisticated devices, the brake to a long electrical cord or tether. All of those controls can fit neatly into a box about the size of a can of Spam, and with today's transistors the box won't weigh more than a paperback book. The bulky power supply remains attached to the layout along with any switch or block controls. There are at least a dozen of these walk-around or hand-held throttles available to any model railroader; some of them sell for less than $20. Most of these throttle controls can be held and operated in just one hand, leaving the other hand free to work switches and power supply toggles or to uncouple cars from the train with a toothpick to move the coupler knuckles. You can now walk alongside your miniature train and have just about the same visual experience as you would driving alongside a real one. That puts you one big step closer to being inside the locomotive's cab.

The closest most of us ever get to being inside a real locomotive is when we happen to be lucky enough to be driving through the country with a train going the same direction as we are. Most of us can only imagine what it would be like to really be inside the locomotive. Walk-around control lets you duplicate the visual experience of "pacing" a train with your automobile, but it adds some touches that make the experience even better with a miniature than with a real train. You are in complete control of that train you're traveling alongside, including both the operation of its locomotive and the operation of the switches into and out of the sidings along the way, *and* you also can control the coupling and uncoupling of the cars. With walk-around control you can be a rail fan traveling along with the train, the engineer, the dispatcher who routes the train and the brakeman or conductor who signals the engineer when to reverse or go forward to couple or uncouple the cars. That puts just about the entire real railroading experience in your hands.

Walk-around control can make a real railroad out of even that 4 x 8-foot toy. First, bolt some extensions on that layout's legs so you don't have that immortal overall view of its pitifully small size. Next, buy a walk-around throttle control with about 15 to 20 feet of cable, and attach it to your power pack. Now you can move that train slowly out of its siding and onto the main line and out and around the table for a complete run over the longest available route—make the whole "day's" run and never get more than a hand's span away from your locomotive. You may have to have some help if you located all those remote-control switch levers on a single panel—shouting or signaling with a real brakeman's hand signals to a "dispatcher" at the switch panel won't do much to shatter the illusion of reality you have by almost living with your train as it moves over the tracks.

Walk-around control suggests some rethinking of traditional wiring concepts. There is really no need for a central control panel. The switches that control track power and move the track switches should be within a couple of feet of the segment of track they control. If the track switches are within a foot

or so of the edge of the layout table, you might want to install manually operated ground-throw-style switch machines like the Alexander or Caboose Industries brands. If the industrial sidings or freight yard tracks are within reach, you might even find it more enjoyable to operate those Kadee couplers by hand. A round toothpick can be used to pry the couplers apart, or buy one of GH Products uncoupling picks, or use one of the plastic Pick-Up Stick game sticks. It's not so difficult to imagine yourself lifting the coupler bar on a real freight car when you move that uncoupling tool to open the coupler knuckles on your models. When such a simple control system can bring you this much closer to bringing what you imagine to life, it's worth devoting a whole chapter to.

The walk-around control system can be used by two engineer/brakeman/dispatcher "operators" if you divide the tracks on your layout into train-length electrical blocks. Cut a gap in the rail and keep it open with some glue. Solder feeder wires from the power supply to that isolated rail, but install a D.P.D.T. Center-Off toggle in the wire with one side of the toggle wired to walk-around throttle A and the other side to throttle B. Turn the D.P.D.T. toggle switch in the direction needed to give the "operator" control, and turn the switch to the center when you want the power off—the proper wiring is illustrated in Volume I. A third "operator" can have control of the yard. With this type of

Fig. 8-2 Just three of the dozens of walk-around or hand-held throttles on the market including Heathkit's (for use only with their power pack) and the MRC Cab Control 55 and Troller Transcab that can be used with most brands of power packs.

Fig. 8-3   If each town has its own control panel with both track power and switch controls, the walk-around concept can be used for either one-man or multiple operator train control.

Fig. 8-4   Lonnie Shay likes the push-button operation of the Mason Locomotive Works walk-around throttle for his HOn3 layout.

wiring system you can have meets between two or more trains that are far more breathtaking than those remote-controlled ones.

The walk-around control system is most effective if you wire the controls to some type of a radio plug like a Cinch-Jones or any four-prong or more type of plug and socket. Put a socket at each town's control panel and wire two walk-around throttles so either one will work with any of the plugs. If you have the D.P.D.T. Center-Off type of control for an A and a B, be sure to provide both an A and a B socket at each control panel. With this type of wiring, the operators of those two meeting trains can both work the same control panel to accomplish their meet before they move on with their trains to the next town. Try to space the control panels and the walk-around throttle sockets so that the walk-around throttle's tether wires don't need to be more than 15 feet long to reach from one town's control panel to the next. The walk-around throttle's plug will have to be plugged and unplugged for you to follow the train around the layout, but few layouts are large enough to require more than one or two such changes, and in any case, it's not much more involved than flicking a toggle switch.

Simplified Wiring Systems

The hobby of model railroading is often just a vehicle for other hobbies or specialties. Many model railroaders are actually rail fans who read about miniatures of real railroads to further their knowledge of the real thing. Some of us are architectural modelers looking for some place to put our miniature buildings. A few of us are electronics hobbyists who find that the practical applications of various control devices are what makes the hobby fascinating. Most of us, though, are trying to find the best way to make a three-dimensional reality—a miniature reality—of railroading. If you're one of those electronics folks, please excuse us all for a moment while we search for some possible ways to get as much real railroading as we can with as little electrical wizardry as possible.

There are a few possibilities of short circuits inherent in the two-rail system. Whenever the right-hand rail crosses the left at a switch or crossing, there is a chance that a short circuit can occur. Shorts are also possible when the tracks are arranged in a reversing loop, a turntable or a wye, because the

very nature of that trackwork is designed to get the right hand rail connected to the left so the trains can be turned. These short circuits can be eliminated permanently by cutting through the rails and filling the cut with some glue to form an insulating gap or, in model railroad terms, a "gap." The general rules and situations in which such gaps must be cut, and the wiring connections around them, are described in Volume I of *The Model Railroading Handbook*. Those basic circuits are all you will need for even the most complex layout design.

WIRING FOR RELIABILITY

One of the major gripes I have with complex wiring and electrical schemes is that they simply offer more places for something to go wrong. I'd rather spend my time getting my locomotives to run smoothly and my trackwork to be derailment free and all of my cars to stay on the track and couple and uncouple reliably. I'd even prefer to have the track switches operated manually with cables and D.P.D.T. switches like those in Volume I, or with the Alexander or Caboose Industries types of ground-throw switch levers shown in Chapter VII. The solonoid types of remote control—called "switch machines" in this hobby—present more potential problems than I want to consider. In any case, wiring diagrams are always furnished with ready-laid remote control switches and with separate switch machines, so there's no point in presenting them here. There are some wires that you should run at every switch to be sure that the electrical current flows where it is supposed to.

Some of the brands of snap-together switches and all of the switch kits and hand-laid switches rely on the switch points to make the electrical contact that carries the current down the route selected by the switch. Model railroad track rails are perfect for carrying current, but they make poor electrical contacts. Dirty and oxidized rail is one bugaboo about model railroading, but it's not much of a bother with nickel silver rail and an

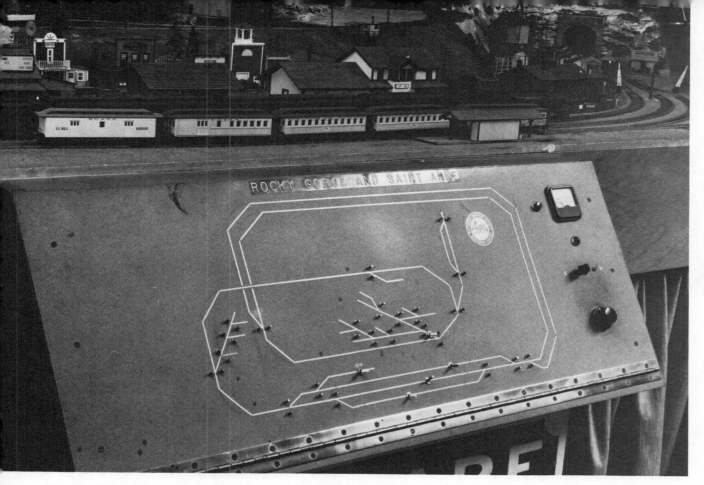

Fig. 9-1   Marshall Nelson has a simple wiring scheme for his two-lap loop layout. The pushbutton controls the switch machines, which also direct the current into the siding or the main line.

occasional wipe over the rail tops with a Bright Boy abrasive pad. The sides of the rails are much harder to clean, and that's the area that switch points must contact to operate the switch. It is, in short, far too easy for there to be poor electrical contact—thanks to dirt, lint, dust, and oxidation forming an insulated area—between the switch points and the rail. The only reliable way to route power through the switch is to have a separate set of contacts that are under the table where less dirt can reach, and where no dirty car wheels can rub them. The D.P.D.T. switch in Volume I serves as that type of contact, and most switch machines have built-in contacts that need only be wired to the rails. The only argument that would convince me to use switch machines is that they do indeed have those built-in contact points.

The wiring diagram shows how a D.P.D.T. switch or the contacts on a switch machine should be wired to the rails of a switch. Please notice that there is absolutely no outside power in this circuit—it's simply a way of insuring that the power to the track switch's rails really does flow on through the switch in the direction the switch is thrown. The D.P.D.T. switch in the diagram is to be mounted beneath the switch and actuated by the same remote cable or rod that moves the switch points. The wires at A and B will only be necessary if you have to cut gaps through the rails near the switch points to avoid short circuits caused by wheels so wide they touch both the open-point rail and its nearest stock rail. This problem is likely to occur only with N scale equipment. If the switch point pivots are loose rail joiners, you should solder some flexible wire to the points and their rails to insure the flow of electricity around those loose joints. In fact, I would recommend that you use jumper wires beneath every single rail joint (except electrical gaps) on your model railroad layout.

Fig. 9-2 The Kemtron (now ADDM) coil-type switch machine has the electrical contacts (left) for routing track power to the siding or main line at the same time the machine moves the switch's point rails.

MULTIPLE TRAIN OPERATION

First, let's define what is meant by operating more than one train at a time. There is relatively little difficulty in operating diesels "mu" or "double-heading" steam locomotives. If you want two or more powered loco-

motives at the head of your train and another pushing behind, the only problem you are likely to encounter with wiring-related items is in having a power pack and throttle with a high enough amperage rating to handle two or more motors. Use an ammeter to check the amperage draw of each of the engines when they are pulling the maximum number of cars you will want them to. Add the readings for all the engines you want to run in one train, and see if that is less than the printed rating on your throttle or power pack. The power packs sold in train sets will only handle one or two locomotives, but most of the $40 and up hobbyist types of power packs have ratings of 2 amps or more, which should be plenty for HO or N scale equipment.

There are more potential problems with the locomotives themselves because each of them must operate within about 2 percent of the speed of the others at every throttle setting. There is next to no chance that you'll get that kind of performance from two or more different brands, and even then there can be a tremendous variation due to wheel or driver size, gearing and even different motor styles. If you are going to operate double-headed

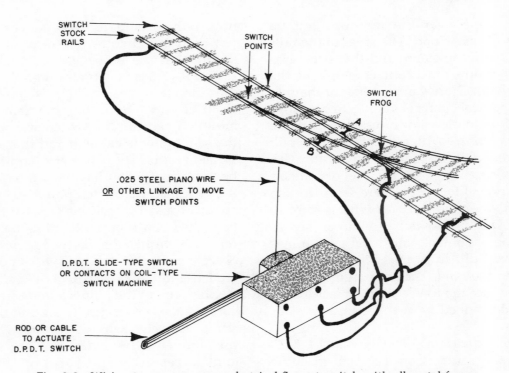

Fig. 9-3 Wiring to ensure proper electrical flow at switch with all-metal frog.

locomotives or use a "helper" at the rear of the train, then all the powered locomotives should be the same brand. You may be able to get those same-brand engines to run closer to each other's speed by giving each of them a tune-up as described in Chapter V. Be sure each of them is as well broken in as the others, and if you still have some performance variations, try increasing or decreasing the motor brush tension on the "slow" locomotive of the set. A little extra lead weight inside the superstructure of one or more of the locomotives can also help to equalize the performance. Be careful with extra weight, however, because the extra traction that results from that weight might allow the motor to overheat (particularly if the locomotive is one with those rubber bands on the wheels or drivers for extra traction).

You can wire your model railroad for the operation of three trains at a time and still use the simple D.P.D.T. Center-Off toggle system. Connect all of the main-line blocks to A and B throttles from the ends of the D.P.D.T. Center-Off switch, but connect the main yard or major town to just one A or B throttle and provide that block with its own throttle. There is little chance that the engineers of both trains A and B will be in the yard at the same time, so either of them can use the blocks with the D.P.D.T. Center-Off switch in the A/B position. The third engineer can continue to operate in the other blocks of the yard. This type of wiring with a separate throttle for the yard is especially helpful for running locomotives in and out of the round-house or engine house and through the other locomotive servicing facilities, while the main-line locomotives are picking up or leaving their trains in the other parts of the yard.

If you have more than two control panels, then two more engineers can operate for every additional panel with a pair of throttle controls. If you use the walk-around type of throttle, then all you will need are sockets for the walk-around throttle plugs and enough walk-around throttles for however many engineers want to run trains at the same time. The practical maximum for a large home layout is about five or six trains and engi-neers; if you have more people than that, assign the extra men to serve as brakemen on the peddler freights and in the yards (to uncouple the cars) and make one a dispatcher.

If you want to operate two trains all by yourself, then set all of the D.P.D.T. Center-Off block switches for train A, adjust the throttle so that second train has enough speed to make it up the hills, and align all of the track switches to that train's route. If you have a layout with an oval as a possible route, that train can circulate for hours with no more attention than an occasional glance from you to see that it's on the rails. If you have a loop-to-loop type of layout, the switches on the reversing loop can be wired to throw automatically and to reverse the current in the loop by using a variation of the signal circuit in this chapter to actuate a switch machine and second relay wired like a D.P.D.T. Center-Off switch. In the meantime you can operate your train by throwing the D.P.D.T. Center-Off switches to B in the blocks occupied by your train. To be safe, turn the blocks on either side of your train to the center-off position so there's no chance of that "automatic" train running into yours. Remember to turn them back to B when you move on to the next block. That type of protection system is almost identical, in principle, to what the real railroads call CTC or Centralized Traffic Control, except that a man (or a computer) in a distant control tower is turning the signal lights and track switches rather than the trains' engineers.

SIGNALING SYSTEMS

Real trains are most often run by diesel engines under the full control of the engineer and fireman. There are some newer override circuits being routed through the rails of some full-size railroads to provide emergency control of the locomotive, but for all practical purposes it is the engineer who controls his locomotive and train. The real railroads use signal lights or signal lights and a semaphore arm to tell the engineer that the track ahead of him is clear. The real railroads call the lengths

Fig. 9-4 In the pre-World War II period, most railroads used signals that were moved by hand levers in control towers. The lever moved a rod through bell crank-type links to change the signal's position.

of track that are protected by those signals "blocks," but that refers more to the distance between each signal rather than the rails themselves. On a model railroad it is convenient to install scale model signals at the gaps for each of our electrical blocks. Those signals can be nonlighted dummies, ones with lights that are always green, ones with lights that change color when the nearest track switch changes direction, or ones that actually show whether or not the next block is clear. The signal is a fine marker to show where the almost invisible gaps are located, and there are several inexpensive brands of plastic signals that will do that job most realistically.

The concept of operating signals can be far more complicated than wiring your model railroad, if you would like it to be. The signals that function like the prototype's must provide a warning that the block *beyond* the next

block is *not* clear (a yellow light or Caution position on a semaphore), whether the very next block is occupied (a red light or a Stop position on a semaphore), or if the next block is clear (a green light or Clear position on a semaphore). A vertical position of the semaphore blade indicates clear, a horizontal position indicates stop, and a 45-degree angle indicates caution. The real railroads often use three or more signals on one post to provide for greater or lesser degrees of caution and/or to show the condition of blocks further down the line. If you want to know what there is to know about signaling, buy John Armstrong's paperback book *All About Signals* for $2 from Kalmbach. We'll settle for a simple green and red one-block system for now.

There are several brands of working signals on the market including NJ Brass, Walthers, LaBelle Industries and AHM. Don Fowler makes a slow-action semaphore. Most of these are HO scale, but the great variance in the sizes of real signals makes most of them suitable for O or S scales. You can convert the N scale plastic signal lights (as well as HO and O scale ones) to illuminated models using small LEDs (light-emitting diodes) or fiber optics kits that are sold by electronics hobby stores like Lafayette and Radio Shack. The better model railroad shops will also be able to order dozens of special solid-state electric circuits and train-detecting systems to help you make that signaling system operate as realistically as the real thing. Just be warned that you'll spend at least as much time playing with electronics and signals as you will with railroads.

THE SIMPLE CIRCUIT

All of the signaling systems, whether for real trains or models, operate on the principle of detecting the train and then translating that into the operation of the signal lights beside the tracks and the identical lights on the dispatcher's control panel in the signal tower. The East/West signaling circuit shown here is one designed and sold by G R Signaling, utilizing parts that can be purchased at any of

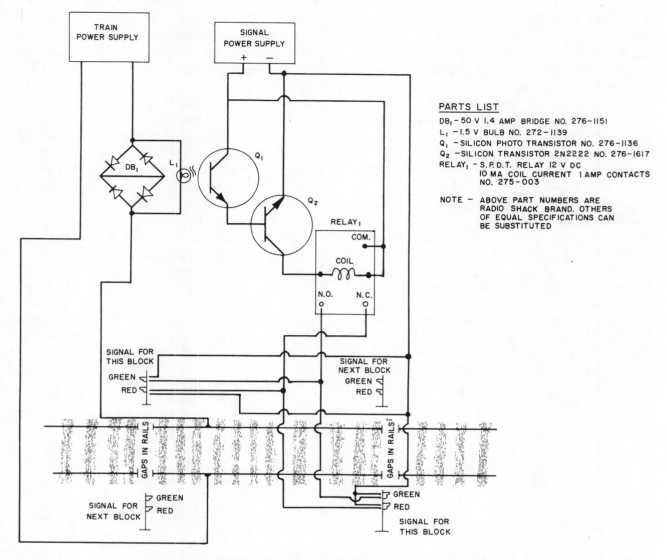

PARTS LIST

DB_1 – 50 V 1.4 AMP BRIDGE NO. 276-1151
L_1 – 1.5 V BULB NO. 272-1139
Q_1 – SILICON PHOTO TRANSISTOR NO. 276-1136
Q_2 – SILICON TRANSISTOR 2N2222 NO. 276-1617
$RELAY_1$ – S.P.D.T. RELAY 12 V DC
          10 MA COIL CURRENT 1 AMP CONTACTS
          NO. 275-003

NOTE – ABOVE PART NUMBERS ARE
       RADIO SHACK BRAND. OTHERS
       OF EQUAL SPECIFICATIONS CAN
       BE SUBSTITUTED

Fig. 9-5 Wiring diagram for east/west signals in one block.

the electronic hobby stores. The part numbers are those used by Radio Shack. The components should run less than $7 plus the cost of wires, signals and signal lights. The circuit is designed to change the signal lights at the entrance of the block from red to green (or vice versa) whenever a locomotive enters the block. This particular circuit is only effective with locomotives whose motors draw 100 milliamps or more. There is no type of electrical contact at the track; it's merely the resistance of the locomotive motor across the track's rails that actuates the circuit.

When a locomotive enters the block, it

Fig. 9-6 Rick Brendel's simplified signal-actuating module made from Radio Shack components. It can also be used for automatic reverse loop or switch machine operation.

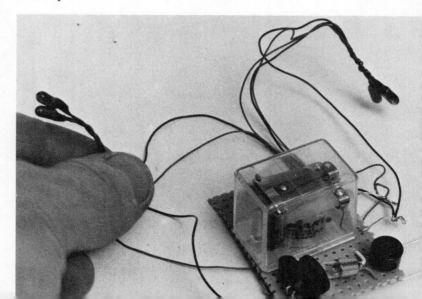

allows enough voltage and current to be drawn through diode bridge 1 to light the light bulb L1. This light falls on photo transistor Q1, which in turn allows current to flow to the base of transistor Q2. Q2 then turns on and passes the voltage to the relay. The relay is energized, and it moves its own contact points to change the track-side signal light bulbs from green to red. When the engine leaves the block, the circuit is interrupted to allow the relay to turn off and pull its own contacts back to the position that changes the track-side signal light from red back to green. You will need one of these units for each block that is equipped with track-side signals. Additional light bulbs can be wired to a dispatcher's control panel to show both the presence of a train and the position or color of the signal light. The relay (or two relays) could be used to move the arm of a semaphore type of signal or to rotate the face of a model of one of the prototype's multibulb

position light signals. The unit will operate with trains in either direction. The relay can be used, as mentioned earlier, to make automatic reverse loop operations and, with some clever wiring, for automatic two-train operations through passing sidings. Use a 10-volt direct-current power supply—an old train set transformer at partial throttle will do—to prolong the life of the light bulbs. The signal light bulbs should be those rated at 12 to 16 volts, but note that the light bulb in the East/West circuit at L1 is 1.5 volts. The diode prevents any more current from reaching that light bulb. The circuit was assembled on a small piece of perforated board from Radio Shack, but you could use masonite or common cardboard. Protect the light bulb's light from straying, and protect the glass itself with a small rubber grommet. All the wire connections should be soldered and wrapped with electrical tape to avoid the chance of a short circuit.

Planning and Operation

There are those who must be called geniuses in any field, and model railroading has had its share. The list could begin with men like Frank Hornby or J. Lionel Cowan, who brought the toy trains to the world, and it would have to include men like the late Frank Ellison, Russ Larson and John Allen. Fortunately, there are people like John Armstrong and W. Allen McClelland who are still alive to contribute to the hobby, and there are at least a dozen others with more on the way. Each of these men has taken some aspect of real railroading and refined it to fit on a model railroad. All of these men are all-around model railroaders with at least enough detail on their individual models to make them realistic, and a rare combination or balance of talents that make their models as worthy of study as the full-size prototypes.

These people have provided a kind of shortcut that we can follow in eliminating the boring business portion of real railroading to distill out only the charm. I have drawn freely on their experience, as they have on each other's, and on the experience of many other model railroaders to present the material in this book and in Volume I. The one thread that ties together all of the men above, except Hornby and Cowan, of course, is their development of operation as another way to get more enjoyment from our hobby. It happens that each of these men also went beyond the prototype to create a name and all the trappings of their own railroads, but that's a story for the next chapter.

Frank Ellison is generally credited with doing more than anyone else to bring real-life railroad operations into the model railroading field. Other men had operated trains as he did, but they lacked his ability to communicate. All of those unsung geniuses that no one has ever heard about out there have only themselves to blame; part of what made Ellison, Larson and Allen and what makes Armstrong and McClelland such superb model railroaders is that each of them was able to communicate his discoveries to the world in magazine articles and books. These men were also willing to learn how to take photographs and to practice the art of writing

Switching Scenarios

so that their ideas could be seen and understood by anyone. Each of these men in their turn has tried to convey almost the same message about lifelike railroading in miniature, and it's valid enough to be told again and again until every novice model railroader understands the real potentials for enjoyment in this hobby.

I can tell their story and show you how others have accomplished similar results, but that's not enough; you have to explore true-to-life operations on your very own model railroad for yourself. Until you have tried it for yourself, believe that a collection of plastic toy trains on snap-together track will seem more real than the best layout in this book *if* those toys are operated like a real railroad. If you have as much as an oval of track and three switches, you can put the lessons of operation from Volume I and from this and the next chapter to work. There's just one problem; these are concepts that are not visible, as a weathered locomotive is visible, and they are not something you can do after seeing them—operating concepts must be learned by study

Fig. 10-1 Switch engines were certainly not the only locomotives that performed switching operations. This is the Ma & Pa's 0-6-0 at Baltimore, Maryland, in September of 1953. (*Photo from the Harold K. Vollrath collection.*)

and by practice before you can understand them. You don't have a McClelland or an Armstrong next door to tutor you, so you're going to have to learn them for yourself by reading and by trying what you read on your layout.

Frank Ellison used the concept of actors, their stage and their stage props and their scripts to explain how to operate a model railroad. This example helped him and his readers to understand that how to operate did not mean how to turn a throttle knob or how to flick a toggle switch or even how to work a coupler. How to operate means how to breath the same kind of life into your railroad that the real railroads have. It's the same hard-to-define feeling of excitement that makes railroads worth modeling—a railroad, unlike a bus terminal or a truck dock or an airport, somehow carries a life of its own with it wherever it goes. Mr. Ellison realized that there was a similar relationship between a stage play and the railroads, in that a really good play brings a life to the stage that is greater than the simple words and motions of the actors and certainly greater than the distorted sets used for stage plays. A play is even better than life, even more real. In the same strange ways, a model railroad can be even more real than real life, but only if it is put into actions at least similar to those of a real railroad.

THE SMALL WORLD OF THE SWITCHER

One of the difficulties with the concepts of the geniuses of the hobby is that the examples they use are model railroads that fill a basement apiece. Each of these men had or has been in the hobby for twenty years, and in that amount of time they have managed to build what can only be called model railroad empires. This gives all us "subjects" an excuse to think that their concepts of model railroad operation are only useful on one of these club-size layouts. That's wrong. It certainly does take some imagination to make two passing sidings on a 5 x 9-foot HO oval simulate four different cities, but imagination is one thing we all have in abundance. It only takes a bit more imagination to envision the one town on a 2 x 4-foot shelf layout as part of a railroad empire. All of the lessons of operation that can be used on a club-sized layout can be used to make that 5 x 9 or 2 x 4 layout better than life. You may not be able to send a 50-car freight flier off on a 200-foot run down an HO scale main line, but you can match the action in at least one of the towns on that hypothetical train's route.

I would recommend that you try to find some way to add enough trackage to a layout to allow at least an oval that might run around behind the backdrop or even out around the front of the layout and behind your back. Support the oval on some fold-up broomstick legs, and anchor it to the main layout with hinges or screws and wing nuts. That oval will help to eliminate one of the things you'd have to imagine, the very existence—not to mention the actual passing through your "town"—of that long-distance traveler. It may seem silly, especially to someone who is modeling a mining or logging line, but that active link with the outside world will make all your other modeling seem more realistic. There's more on this subject in the next chapter; for now, let's concentrate on what's happening in town during those lulls between the cross-country fliers.

One of the things that gives a railroad life is

that we are aware that it is carrying many of the goods we need to survive. Part of that feeling stems from the turn of the century, when the railroad was often the only link with the outside world. The feeling is reinforced even today, when you realize how dependent a city (where most of us live) is on the nightly deliveries of, for example, food to the supermarkets. Although that food is delivered in trucks, many of those trucks pulled trailers that were flying through the night on one of the TOFC TrailerTrain flat cars just a few hours ago. In all likelihood, a switch engine pushed that flat car into its siding last night, just as an engine pushed similar flat cars with trailers and boxcars and reefers into sidings in almost every town in America. When you duplicate that action of switching cars in and out of sidings, you are duplicating an important part of each of our life cycles. You can bypass another of those imagination pitfalls by making a "bill of lading" for the goods that are being loaded or unloaded from that car—a system of "cargo" cards that's much easier to use than the rules of a monopoly game as described in Volume I. The im-

Fig. 10-2 The run-around is one of the basic switching movements. This peddler freight is going to pick up that Burlington boxcar and leave the Shell tank car in its place on the siding.

Fig. 10-3 The locomotive set uncouples from the train, heads forward to clear the switch on the double-ended (passing) siding, then backs to clear the points on the switch on the opposite end of the siding.

Fig. 10-4 The locomotive moves forward to couple to the rear of the train and push it forward enough so the Shell tank car will clear the boxcar's siding. The tank car is then left in its position.

Fig. 10-5　The train is reversed and moves far enough to clear the points on the box-car's siding. The train then moves forward into the boxcar's siding and couples to the boxcar.

Fig. 10-6　The locomotive pulls the train—now with the boxcar—back enough to clear the switch. The train is then pushed forward to couple onto the tank car and the tank car is backed, then pushed into the siding. The locomotive then runs back around the train to couple back onto the front to proceed forward to the next town.

portant point is that you be aware that that car contains or will contain some commodity; it's not merely a Union Pacific boxcar anymore.

The bill of lading card and the name of the industry and the type of car will tell you why to move that car in or out of a siding. The purpose of this chapter is to show you how that move is made on the real railroads. If the car and the siding are behind the engine with the siding trailing away toward the caboose, then all you have to do is uncouple the train just ahead of that car so you can back it into the siding. When the siding's switch is facing the direction of your train's travel, then you must execute the run-around maneuver shown in the photographs to be able to get behind the car to get it into the facing siding. Every switching move is based on one of these two concepts. That cross-country flier train enters into the maneuver because you have to be aware of its existence and the existence of all other trains when you let your switching engine venture out from the siding onto the main line for that run-around maneuver.

If you understand that the switching maneuvers are ways of getting life-support commodities to the world, you can almost forget that those are railroad cars. You'll begin to feel that they are actually hauling something. Then you are not just pushing around a boxcar with a locomotive, you're completing an essential part of modern life. The existence of that cross-country flier helps to put your switching work into perspective as being but a portion of the role the railroads play in life. The railroads are run by men and women who, like you, work those throttles and brakes and couplers that they need to make many separate cars into a train. The switching moves and the passing of that flier are examples of living railroads that happen to use locomotives, rolling stock track, structures and earth itself that you have put there.

Placing a Union Pacific boxcar on that piece of HO scale track is a very small part of what it takes to make a model of a real railroad. It certainly doesn't take a model of the entire state of Arizona to make a real railroad model; the essence of real railroading can be captured in as little as 2 x 4 feet with models of any scale. It's interesting to know that this model railroader's hall of fame members like Frank Ellison, John Allen, Paul Larson, Allen McClelland and John Armstrong all created their own railroad names rather than pick a particular prototype railroad. These men knew something that you and I don't; in fact they knew many things we could learn.

According to what they have written, all of them had similar reasons why they did not select a particular real railroad but chose to create their own. The real railroads they liked just didn't offer the exact kind of locomotives, cars and scenery they wanted for their models. These men knew so much about applying real railroad practices to their models that they could go beyond reality to create a model railroad that was as real as any. Don't let your ego carry you far enough to think you should create your own road for the same reasons they did. The creation of a new railroad is no shortcut to a better model railroad; it's far more likely to be a way of being too lazy to learn what you should to make your railroad accurate.

The approach that these men took to creating their railroads is the same path that you should follow for any model railroad; describe what your portion of, say, the Santa Fe will be and how you will operate it. Real railroads have a habit of only fulfilling a portion of our fantasies about them. I happen to find the Colorado Midland fascinating enough to have selected it as the prototype for my own modeling endeavors. I've read everything I could find on the subject. I belong to the Colorado Midland Modelers Club, so I can tell them what I've discovered about the railroad and the easiest ways to model it and its equipment, and I can learn what the other members have discovered. I've also read what I can about the railroads that the CM had to compete with, and I've even visited the por-

Modeling Real Railroads

tion of the railroad I would like to model. There is, however, a problem with my choice of prototypes; I happen to like real railroading from the 1900s right through to the 1950s, and the Colorado Midland was abandoned in 1923! That presents a dilemma: I can ignore almost half of the real trains I like, or I can build a model railroad based on what might have happened to the CM if it had survived. Even one of the most perfect prototypes for a model railroad isn't good enough.

The Maryland & Pennsylvania Railroad has long been a favorite prototype for model railroaders, for many of the same reasons that the Colorado Midland is such a fine choice: these railroads are small enough to be almost "model" railroads in their own right. They operate through hills and mountains like the ones we use to give excuses for the curves and tunnels we need to keep our tracks from running off the edges of the table. Their major yards were small enough so they can be modeled with just a little "selective compression" (see the following section) and their rosters of cars and locomotives could be duplicated al-

Fig. 11-1 The Colorado Midland's Colorado City roundhouse—all 14 stalls of it—in HO scale. The roundhouse is a Model Masterpieces kit, built and photographed by Donald Meeker.

most in their entirety within the twenty years or so it takes to complete a really extensive model railroad. In the interim, small segments of the railroad and individual examples of its locomotives and rolling stock could be built. It doesn't matter all that much whether that twenty-year goal of a full roster is completed, just as long as it's a possibility.

The Ma & Pa was one of the last railroads to operate the small steam locomotives of the twenties and the turn-of-the-century periods. Model railroaders noticed the line in the fifties, and soon brass locomotives and decals and magazine articles on models of its equipment began to appear regularly. It's been more than twenty years, and I know of only one modeler who has even attempted to actu-

ally model the Ma & Pa; Bud Sima has a yard that duplicates most of the feeling of the line's Baltimore facility and an extensive railroad with Ma & Pa flavor. The track plan in Chapter XIII is the first one that has reduced the principal features of the line to model railroad proportions. If the railroad is so well worth modeling, why has only one modeler done so? The answer is fairly simple. The closer you look at any particular real railroad and the more you learn about it, the more you realize that it has made compromises you don't have to make. When you know that, then you're ready to go on to improve on reality. If you want a really effective model railroad, with the elusive flavor that gives life to the real thing, then you must start with the real thing. Pick a prototype, try to reduce its essence to fit your space, and then change what you must to make it suit you. When you have done that, you can actually plan your layout and pick your structures, locomotives and rolling stock, so the whole can be greater than the sum of its parts, a railroad that can be operated and experienced as though it were real.

COLORADO CITY, COLORADO, FEBRUARY 1900

The 4 x 6-foot diorama of an HO scale model of the Colorado Midland's Colorado City engine-servicing area is one example of reducing a real railroad to HO scale. The diorama includes an exact scale model of the Colorado City roundhouse and turntable, but the machine shop and the nearby tracks are very much reduced as compared to the prototype. It's one way to use the technique known as selective compression, by which a real-life structure or scene is foreshortened in its

overall dimensions rather than being built as a precise-scale model.

The Athearn HO scale all-plastic "heavyweight" passenger cars and their streamlined cars (except for the baggage car) are some other examples; these cars are exact HO scale in every dimension but length. The 80-foot prototypes for these models were duplicated, but with about 20 scale feet removed from the centers of the cars. The shorter cars capture the general feeling of the real thing without being too long for layouts with 18-inch radius curves. The streamlined baggage car in the series, like many head-end passenger cars, was shorter on the prototype, so it was modeled full-length and the other cars shortened to match it. You'll see the same type of concept applied to the York and Baltimore yards on the Ma & Pa track plan in Chapter XIII; the main features—including full-scale turntables, engine house and roundhouse—are all there, but the length and the number of the sidings have been reduced.

The Model Masterpieces diorama was built to display that firm's Colorado City round-

Fig. 11-2 The usual debris of barrels, ties and scrap surrounds the Colorado City roundhouse on the Model Masterpieces 4 x 6-foot diorama. (*Photo by Donald Meeker, Courtesy of Model Masterpieces Ltd.*)

Fig. 11-3   An example of selective compression as applied to the Colorado City round-house—four stalls and the stonework effectively capture the spirit of the prototype in just a fraction of the space. (*Photo by Donald Meeker, Courtesy of Model Masterpieces Ltd.*)

house kit and their machine shop. Their roundhouse, however, is available with as few as four stalls, and it still captures much of the feeling of the prototype. Many modelers prefer locomotives above everything else in the hobby, and an almost half-circle round-house is just what will make them happy, even more so if it's an exact-scale replica of a real one. It's really a space-wasting idea, but this is, after all, a hobby in which we can indulge ourselves in any way we please when it comes to the use of space. I have said much about various rules for model railroading. Those rules are meant to be broken whenever that will increase your modeling pleasure. You'll find that I have left out about four of the Baltimore yard tracks on the Ma & Pa plan and shortened the ones that I did keep, just to get the space for all 11 stalls of that fine round-house on the real railroad. I wouldn't want to model the Ma & Pa without it.

The only way to achieve a realistic model railroad is to study the prototype and apply everything you can learn to your railroad in miniature. Try to avoid the mistake of making an entire model railroad layout and then trying to find some prototype or prototypes that will fit it. I have listed several real railroads that could be used on the Ma & Pa layout instead of the Maryland & Pennsylvania and the Baltimore & Ohio railroads it was designed to

duplicate. Here it's a case of finding a real railroad concept that happens to be applicable to other real railroads. A large number of modelers are building narrow-gauge railroads in miniature, and one reason for their choice of that type of prototype is that the real narrow-gauge lines were often back-woods logging or mining roads that had to make do with whatever used equipment they could find. This kind of prototype leaves the modeler the freedom to do likewise and make custom locomotives and cars without having to worry about whether or not there is a prototype. There's nothing wrong with that type of modeling if the modeler takes the time and trouble to do some extensive research on what the real logging and mining railroads did. Some of the most realistic model railroads in the country are built on this concept. Again, the choice of not modeling a prototype is not a shortcut but the result of searching through enough prototype information to know what can be kept and what can be discarded to maintain realism.

MODELING A TYPICAL APPALACHIAN SHORT LINE

I've selected the Maryland & Pennsylvania as one of the best possible prototypes for a

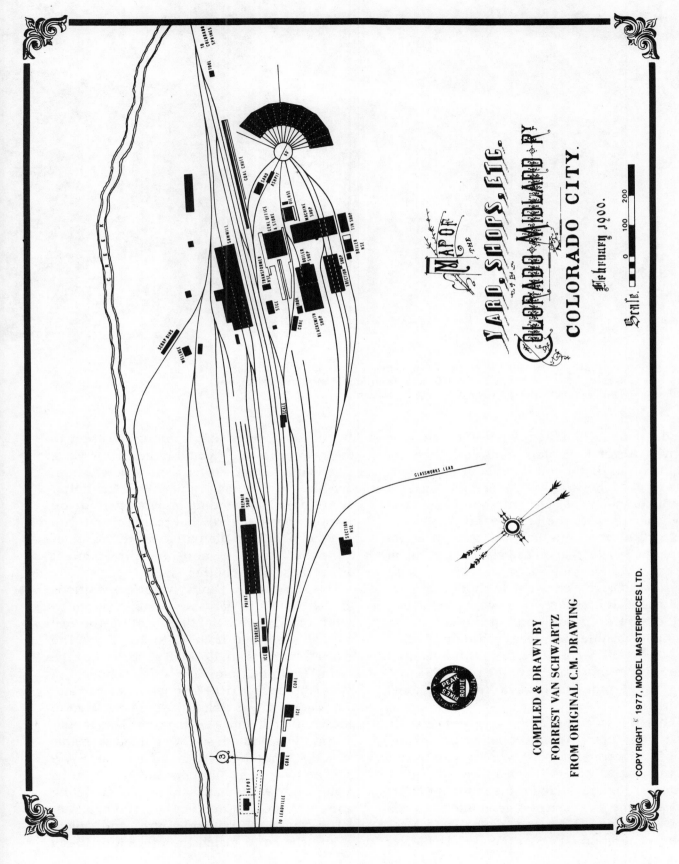

Fig. 11-4 Colorado City, on the Colorado Midland, in 1900 would take a room at least 10 x 30 feet if modeled in HO scale. The Model Masterpieces diorama captures the effect in just 4 x 6 feet. (Model Masterpieces drawing by Forrest Van Schwartz.)

Fig. 11-5 One wall was left off the machine shop on the Colorado City diorama to show the interior. All of the machinery is HO scale from Model Masterpieces castings and kits. (*Photo by Donald Meeker, Courtesy of Model Masterpieces Ltd.*)

model railroad. You'll see some of the reasons why in several chapters. This line, like the Colorado Midland and just about any other, has its own shortcomings. When the Ma & Pa went diesel, it selected only one basic style switcher. In fact, the line has an SW-1, two NW-2 and SW-9 engines, but it takes a real expert to tell them apart at a glance. The steam locomotives are gone and have been for about two decades. If you want to model the real railroad as it is today, you're going to have to settle for a pretty dull diet of diesels. If you want to include the steam locomotives that made the 1955-era Ma & Pa so interesting, then you cannot use any of the post-1955 rolling stock and still have a credible model railroad.

There are two outs at the very least: decide that some new industry opened up on the line—perhaps at Dallastown so you won't have to actually model such a giant—has provided enough revenue for the railroad to purchase some heavier first-generation diesels like GP-7s or SD-24s and maybe even a second-generation GP-35 or the like. The Ma &

Pa paint scheme is simple enough to apply to the newer diesels. If you'd rather, your Ma & Pa could lease the newer motive power from the B&O, the Pennsylvania, Penn Central or even Conrail, depending on what period you want to consider and what paint scheme you like best. Either alternative is the kind of thing that a full-size short-line railroad might do, because many of them have.

The Maryland & Pennsylvania's operations in the state of Maryland were abandoned south of Whiteford in 1958, cutting the real railroad's mileage from 77 to about 35. The Conrail mergers in 1976 left a portion of the Penn Central from York-Walkersville (in Maryland) to Fredrick, Maryland, isolated and the Ma & Pa was able to use its trackage to add another 50 miles to its route. This revitalization was enough so the railroad was able to add yet another NW-2 and another SW-9 pair of switchers (numbers 84 and 85) to its roster and, with thanks from the modeling fraternity, a GP-7 (number 86). The new diesels received the railroad's black and yellow paint scheme to match the other four diesel switchers. That still doesn't provide the "second generation" diesels some modelers would prefer, but there's always the chance that those 1940-era switchers might be replaced with some larger line's hand-me-down diesels. You'll still have to find an excuse for the existence of the Baltimore yard after 1958, but it wouldn't take much of a twist in the Ma & Pa's "storybook" history for that to have actually happened.

When a model railroader with some extensive knowledge of the prototype railroads encounters some features of his or her favorite that he or she just doesn't want to model, there are some interesting ways to solve the dilemma and still stick with what is called prototype practice. Let's use the Maryland & Pennsylvania again; it never really carried enough passengers to invest in the heavy-weight steel passenger cars let alone in streamliners. To some, the open-platform wood cars are a primary reason for picking the line.

What if you'd like to see some all-mail trains, or operate some passenger trains that set out and pick up dining cars or sleepers or baggage cars and you still want to model the Ma & Pa? Well, do so, but remember what the prototype is like and limit your cars to coaches and head-end cars that, model or prototype, were less than 72 feet long so they would be able to negotiate the railroad's sharp curves. You'll have to forego the diner and sleeping car, but you could substitute some milk cars or Railway Express cars to allow some passenger train switching. Here is where you have to draw the line; if you must have streamliners or those 80-footers from the

Fig. 11-6   Few of the preelectricity machine shops survive. Steam engines turned overhead jackshafts, and belts drove the machines. They still did in 1972 at Yakima, Washington.

Fig. 11-7   The Maryland & Pennsylvania's "common" four-window center-cupola wood caboose was modified, in the case of number 2002, with a side door. (*Photo from the J. E. Murphy collection, circa 1965.*)

Fig. 11-8   One of the fascinations about the Ma & Pa as a "model" model railroad prototype is the fact that it really did have a total of four four-wheel cabooses. (*Photo from the Harold K. Vollrath collection, circa 1951.*)

steel era, then pick some other real railroad for your prototype, even though it doesn't match the character of the Ma & Pa—an absolute fact you wouldn't know without a pretty thorough study of the prototype railroad.

There are other ways to reconstruct a prototype railroad to suit your needs for a "model" for your model railroad. A model railroader is far more likely to find passenger trains interesting than the real railroad managers did. Passenger trains were operated at a loss by most real railroads from about 1930 until Amtrak took over. Some prototypes with interesting yards, structures and locomotives hauled little but logs or iron ore, so even the freight cars on a model of one of those roads would be dull.

You might consider creating a subsidiary line for the real railroad that would have a different name but the same paint scheme and the same steam locomotive styles. Many real railroads had subsidiaries like the Burlington's Colorado & Southern or Fort Worth & Dodge lines or the Southern Pacific's Cotton

Belt. There are enough examples to make it prototype practice even if your favorite didn't actually practice it. If my beloved Colorado Midland had survived, it would very likely have become a subsidiary of the Colorado & Southern or even the Santa Fe—both real railroads owned the CM for a while. I'd pick the Burlington and settle for the 1955 era, when both steam and diesel locomotives operated and the Burlington had just begun to paint its grey and black diesels red and grey. I'd letter them Burlington along with all the cabooses and freight cars, but with the small letters "CM" in place of the "CB&Q" just as the C&S and the FW&D did. If I were to place the Colorado Midland in the Appalachians, I'd probably pick the New York Central for a prototype and, like the Pittsburgh & Lake Erie, I'd add my Central Midland CM letters to the NYC's steam and diesel locomotives and rolling stock.

Your rolling stock must match the prototype you pick as well. If you have to have both a logging railroad and a railroad that

Fig. 11-9 An example of the boxcars in the Ma & Pa's 1000 through 1020 series. It is probably painted grey with black lettering just for this 1910 builders photo from the J. E. Murphy collection.

hauls conventional rolling stock, then find a real one that does both, like the Washington, Idaho & Montana in Idaho. This railroad follows more or less Milwaukee Road lines—it now leases one of their diesels—but it owned its own 10-wheelers and consolidations and Mikados. If you want a line that was powered by Shays, Heislers and other geared locomotives, you'll have to look elsewhere.

If you do decide on a real railroad like the Burlington, then be very sure to include enough of those identical batches of freight cars to convey that character of the real railroad. The CB & Q and its C & S subsidiary haul a lot of coal, including several of the modern "unit" trains that never uncouple from the mine to the power station or Great Lakes car dumpers. Both railroads carried a lot of beef in the pre-1955 periods, so strings of stock cars would be part of that kind of scene. Don't waste your money on reefers, at

least until you have several sets of a dozen boxcars, hoppers and stock cars with "Q" lettering; if it's reefers you like, then pick the Santa Fe or the Southern Pacific or the Union Pacific with their bright orange and yellow cars. If I were modeling one of these railroads, I'd have to stop the clock at about 1957 so I could include a foreshortened (by selective compression) train-length icing platform in the middle of nowhere like those on the Union Pacific, where every train of reefers had to stop for a few hours to be reiced.

BRIDGE TRAFFIC

The major mistake that model railroaders make is to try to include an entire railroad on their layout. There is a tendency for a newcomer to think that his or her railroad will seem more realistic if every train starts in one

Fig. 11-10   The Maryland & Pennsylvania 4-6-0s number 27 and 28 were almost identical when built. The rods for the outside valve gear, the cooling coil pipes and the steel sheathing over the wood cab were added later. (*Photo from the Harold K. Vollrath collection, circa 1939.*)

Fig. 11-11   Ma & Pa consolidations (2-8-0s) number 23, 24, 25 and 26 are the most famous locomotives in HO scale thanks to thousands of brass ready-to-run replicas. Number 26 displays the steel sheathing applied to the wood cabs in the thirties. (*Photo from the Harold K. Vollrath collection, circa 1942.*)

big yard and ends in another. It might also seem that it would be realistic to have as many source-to-consumer sets of industries as possible so you and your visitors could see the logs being hauled to the sawmill, lumber to the lumberyard or box factory and boxes to the furniture factory, etc. There isn't even room on a *real* railroad for that complete a cycle! It's in the same category as trying to add a complete seaport or airport or steel mill to a 5 x 9-foot layout when any one of those by itself is too large for that much space even in N scale. This again is where a knowledge of the real railroads' operations is helpful and particularly a knowledge of the railroad you are using as your model.

Most real railroads survive because they haul carloads of materials *from* other railroads they connect with *to* other railroads they connect with, or at the very least connect one of their line-side industries with the outside world. About 95 percent of the freight shipments and much of the passenger traffic on your railroad should probably be coming from or going to someplace that is not on your layout. If you must have two yards, like the Ma & Pa layout, then remember to include some tracks where your yards connect with other railroads, as they do on the real ones and on the model Ma & Pa. With the exception of a few seaports and the woods end of some logging railroads and branch lines, the yards on a real railroad are one of the major places where foreign freight cars are sorted for delivery to and from customers along the railroad. When those cars are merely to be routed over the railroad from a customer on some other line and to a customer on a third line, that traffic is called bridge traffic because it uses the middle railroad as a bridge route between the other two. All the middle railroad has to do is pick the car up in one

Fig. 11-12   The number 21 and 22 10-wheelers were the oldest on the Ma & Pa; the Pennsylvania Railroad built them as part of their G-2 class in 1881. (*Photo from the Harold K. Vollrath collection, circa 1900.*)

yard and drop it off in another. The railroad that owns the car can, however, charge the middle railroad rent for the time that car spends on its rails, so bridge traffic is moved as quickly as possible. If you have the nerve to do it, plan that perfect layout with no yards at all, and use the space you save for scenery and small towns where you can have some better switching action among small industries. If you have just the space for a 2 x 4-foot layout with one town, then the knowledge that most of the traffic on the railroads to and from that town is bridge traffic can make your operating times feel much more realistic.

Every model railroad that has ever been made has been a one-of-a-kind creation of its builder. There have been hundreds of duplicates of what you can do with 18-inch radius snap-together track on a piece of 4 x 8-foot plywood, but even those are different from one another when the structures are added. A lot of armchair model railroaders spend years searching through the monthly magazines and through books to find that perfect layout plan. Don't bother, because that plan exists only in your own imagination. I'd like to show you how to pry that secret from yourself so you can get started on your dream layout this weekend.

For the first step in planning your layout please flip back a few pages and reread the last two chapters. You can keep that dream layout from becoming a nightmare by picking a prototype and knowing exactly why you picked what you did. You have probably selected the scale you like best by now, but please forget it for a moment and listen to the wisdom of others. The scale you select for your model railroad should be one that will allow you to squeeze the kind of a prototype you prefer in the amount of space you have for a miniature of that prototype. If you really want to operate 80-foot and longer passenger cars and you only have 5 x 9 feet of space, then N scale is your only logical choice. If you have to have HO scale in that area, then build a couple of 2 x 4-foot modules and hope you can find a club or some other people, so that together you can operate a multimodule layout. If the module concept doesn't appeal to you, then consider changing your prototype for a freight-only railroad or for an earlier period when 70-foot and shorter passenger cars were common.

You should know that there is virtually no model railroad in the land that has not been compromised in a manner similar to those I've mentioned. Somehow there is never quite as much space or time or money as you think there is. If you'll pay attention, though, you can make most of those compromises before you even lift a pencil, instead of waiting until you've laid all the track. Curves are the major obstacles you'll face when designing any model railroad. The real railroads have very, very broad-radius curves; the Maryland & Pennsylvania is known for its tight curves, but the sharpest of those is a whopping 39-inch radius if reduced to HO scale. The standard-gauge Rio Grande Western snakes through the Rockies with curves no tighter than an HO scale 65-inch radius! No wonder that 86-foot piggyback flat cars and 80-foot passenger cars look strange on those 18-inch radius curves.

The members of the National Model Railroad Association have done a lot of research about curves for model trains; I'd suggest you join and read the figures on the "Recommended Practices" number RP 11 that you'll receive as part of your membership. You'll find—either by believing the chart or by the bitter experience of building too-tight curves for yourself—that an 18-inch radius in HO scale is only enough for the operation of 60-foot passenger cars (only the 1880-era open-platform cars were that short), small consolidations like Ma & Pa number 25 and diesels with four-wheel trucks. Any modern

Planning Your Own Layout

Fig. 12-1   The streets and structures of a city can disguise a lack of planning, but they don't make operation very interesting.

Fig. 12-2   The slight S-bend and two sidings on this simple double track oval layout add to the realism with a minimum of complication.

equipment should be operated on curves of about 32 inches. You can squeeze a few inches off those numbers by installing easements at the ends of all curves to make the change from straight to curve less of a lurch, but 26 inches is about the practical minimum radius for HO scale. If you want less, you have to go to Gay Nineties period prototypes, to a logging operation or to HO narrow gauge. An 18-inch radius is a similar minimum for N scale, and 58 inches is about the minimum radius for O scale.

The narrow-gauge prototypes are more popular than ever because they allow the use of a fairly large model on relatively sharp curves. Why? Because the real-life narrow-gauge equipment is about ⅔ to ¾ the size of standard gauge and so are the minimum practical curve radii. The most popular narrow-gauge prototypes are the ones with a 3-foot spacing between the tops of the rails that ran in Colorado's Rockies. Most HOn3 layouts have models of the Rio Grande, Rio Grande Southern, or the Colorado & Southern railroads' locomotives and rolling stock. There are many kits and ready-built brass models of similar prototypes in On3.

HOn30″ is probably the next most popular narrow-gauge choice. These models are built to HO scale but with trackwork, chassis and trucks from N scale equipment which, if measured with an HO scale ruler, checks out to be about 30 inches between the rail heads. The 2-foot-gauge lines that ran in Maine were close enough to 30 inches for most modelers. HO scale trackwork, locomotive chassis and trucks are about right for 24-inch or 2-foot-gauge models in O scale, so On2 is one of the other popular scales. HO items are also very close, 3½-feet in S scale, so some modelers are building Sn3½ layouts with HO trackwork, chassis and trucks or in Sn3 with respaced wheels. There are several kits and many castings for dead-accurate On2 and Sn3 equipment, and a few modelers elect to build their own locomotives, track and trucks to exact-scale track gauges. In general, the NMRA-recommended 18-inch radius for HO scale old-time equipment is fine for HOn3, Sn3 or On2, and 9 inches is enough for

HOn30″ or HOn2. On3 locomotives can usually make it around 24-inch radius curves.

If your compromises with prototype, space, minimum radius and scale and track gauge are settled, you're ready to get on with some more advanced layout prethinking. Do not try to convince yourself that you can build an O-shaped layout where you must duck under something to get at the controls—the lift bridges and swing-up track sections that allow access to such a layout are never as easy to use as you think they are, so you end up ducking under them and hating yourself for ever thinking of the idea. The ideal layout is one located on a shelf 24 to 30 inches wide around the walls of a room, but there can be problems if you ever have to move, because you'll probably never find other walls just that length.

A compromise is the type of a layout with a shelf along two walls and a peninsula about 2 feet or more from the third and fourth walls. The Ma & Pa layout in the next chapter is designed for just that situation in a two-car garage, or you can make your own room within a room, as Lonnie Shay did for his 15′ x 15′ HOn3 layout in his two-car garage. You will not be able to reach much more than 30 inches from the edge of the layout, so an island-style layout like the typical 4′ x 8′ or 5′ x 9′ really must have at least an 18-inch access aisle on each side. That access means that a 5′ x 9′ island layout like Figure 12-6 will actually require about 7½′ x 11½′ of floor space to provide a minimum 2-foot aisle on one side and end and an 18-inch aisle along the rear. You could build up to AA of the layout in Figure 12-7 with just another foot of space and have a much more desirable layout. If the layout in Figure 12-7 is shortened, the passing sidings between the two AA lines can be rotated 90 degrees to fit along the back wall. There will also have to be an 18-inch or wider aisle at the right end of the loop.

These layout plans offer the basic trackage that can be squeezed into the minimum areas shown with 24-inch minimum-radius curves and number 6 switches. Virtually every layout plan you'll ever see is a variation or complication of one of these basic designs.

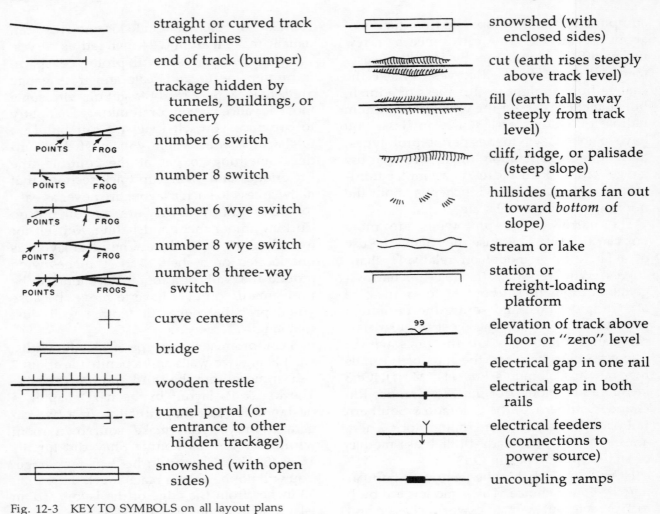

Fig. 12-3   KEY TO SYMBOLS on all layout plans

The symbols include:

- straight or curved track centerlines
- end of track (bumper)
- trackage hidden by tunnels, buildings, or scenery
- number 6 switch (POINTS, FROG)
- number 8 switch (POINTS, FROG)
- number 6 wye switch (POINTS, FROG)
- number 8 wye switch (POINTS, FROG)
- number 8 three-way switch (POINTS, FROGS)
- curve centers
- bridge
- wooden trestle
- tunnel portal (or entrance to other hidden trackage)
- snowshed (with open sides)
- snowshed (with enclosed sides)
- cut (earth rises steeply above track level)
- fill (earth falls away steeply from track level)
- cliff, ridge, or palisade (steep slope)
- hillsides (marks fan out toward *bottom* of slope)
- stream or lake
- station or freight-loading platform
- elevation of track above floor or "zero" level (99)
- electrical gap in one rail
- electrical gap in both rails
- electrical feeders (connections to power source)
- uncoupling ramps

Fig. 12-4   KEY TO LETTERS on all layout plans

A   connecting ends of hidden storage siding
B   connecting ends of hidden storage siding
C   connecting ends of hidden storage siding
CI   cinder pit for steam locomotives to dump spent fires
CT   coaling tower or trestle used for re-fueling locomotives
E   engine house or roundhouse
FRT   freight house for less than carload lot (lcl) freight
O   lubricating and fuel oil storage

OFF   yard office
STA   station
TT   turntable
W   water tower
X   trackage used for reversing on double-track main line or for "long" run from York to Baltimore
Y   trackage used for reversing on double-track main line or for "long" run from York to Baltimore
Z   trackage used for reversing on double-track main line or for "long" run from York to Baltimore

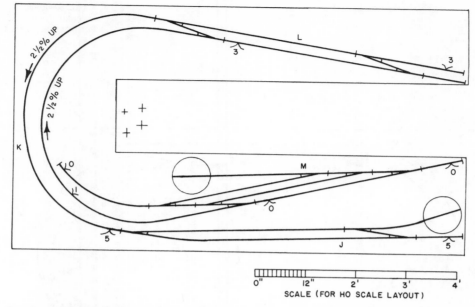

Fig. 12-5   BASIC LAYOUT I: an HO scale point-to-point walk-in layout for a 5 x 9-foot area.

The loop-to-loop plan in Figure 12-8 is probably the best of the lot for most model railroader's needs, in that it provides a maximum amount of trackage with the prototype-like point-to-point operation, but with room for a reversing loop at each terminal so trains can be run nonstop when desired. True point-to-point railroads like Figure 12-7 can become tiresome after a few years of back-and-forth operation, especially when friends want to see the trains run.

The switchback type of layout in Figure 12-5 is best-suited to a logging or mining prototype or to one of the very small short-line railroads. I've included a turntable at each terminal of this layout to give your train crews a bit more to do, but there's no real need for them because the train is going to be backing up for half of its trip regardless. The layout in Figure 12-6 is really for experienced modelers used to working with grades and tight clearances. It has too much track, but it makes a pretty decent plan if the terminals J and M can be located on shelves of their own; if you do, keep the loops so you can still have continuous operation when you want to.

Any of these basic track plans can be mirrored to suit your space and the location of the doorway into the layout room. Each of them would be a much better layout if even a foot were added in any direction, or even better, if they were built with N scale equipment and trackwork or HOn3 or HOn30" or On2 trackwork and equipment. The Ma & Pa layout in the next chapter is an example of how the plan in Figure 12-8 can be developed into a double-track main line. The single-track portion of the Ma & Pa plan is really just a point-to-point version of Figure 12-8 superimposed over the double-track main line, but with a few extra switches for some variations on either theme.

PLANNING FOR OPERATION

The track plans in this chapter indicate some of the time-proven basic paths that the tracks can follow to squeeze as much scale mileage as possible from a minimum amount of space. When you're designing your own layout, keep reminding yourself that you want to stick to that favorite prototype railroad you've researched so thoroughly. If you really do want to run modern 80 and 86-foot cars in HO scale, then the mini-

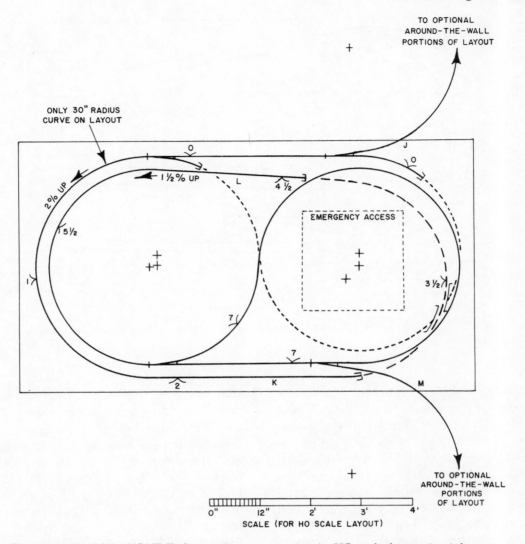

Fig. 12-6   BASIC LAYOUT II: for maximum operation in HO scale from a 5 x 9-foot area.

mum-radius curves will have to be increased, so that these layouts will require about another 20 percent more space in both directions.

The layout in Figure 12-8 is the only one that will give you the operations you will likely want if you want modern equipment. The layouts in Figures 12-6 and 12-7 are best suited to 1920s or earlier period railroads, narrow-gauge or trolley operations, just because the main lines are so short. Notice that none of these plans have space for a yard. That's a space-gobbling luxury that will require another 2 x 8-feet of space (for HO scale equipment) somewhere beyond the con-

fines of these layouts. Please give some serious considerations to leaving the yard out if you are that cramped for space and instead have a "fiddle" yard or a hidden storage yard.

This preplanning period is the time to decide on train lengths too. The sidings I have included are about 4 feet long, which means you can have trains that long plus the length of the locomotive. The locomotive will run around the train for switching, or if the train is being passed by another train, its locomotive can uncouple and duck into an industrial siding until the pass is complete. Four feet is only room enough for four 80-foot passenger

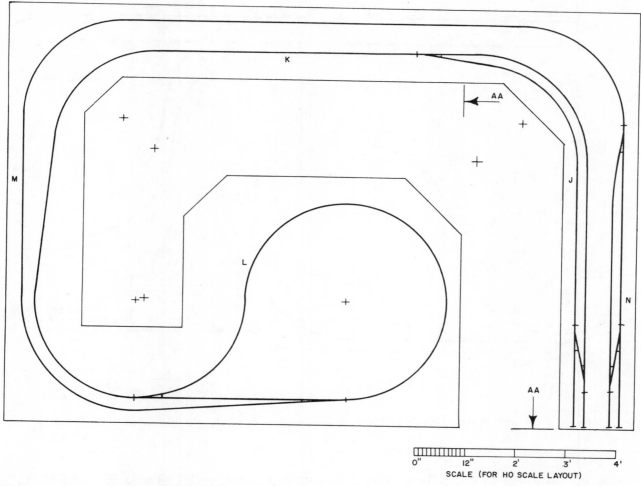

Fig. 12-7 BASIC LAYOUT III: HO scale point-to-point walk-around layout for 8½ x 9 or 8½ x 12½-foot area.

cars or three 86-foot modern freight cars and a caboose or for five 60-foot cars and a caboose or for seven 40-foot cars and a caboose or for eight 34-foot cars and a caboose. You can get a lot more railroading action in a given amount of space by picking one of the earlier periods for your layout. You can also see just how much space a 4-foot passing siding takes by looking at the sidings J and L on Figure 12-5 (sidings M are just 30 inches) and siding N on Figure 12-7. The longer sidings will use up most of the main line, and even worse, those longer trains' cabooses will barely have left one "town" before their locomotives arrive in the next.

If you're still stuck on long or modern trains, then reconsider the use of N scale or NTRAK or even one of the HO or On3 module concepts. Almost any of the 18-inch-wide wall shelves on these layouts could be made wider and the track routed to correspond with the module specifications in just that area. You wouldn't be able to enjoy very long trips with your long trains at home, but you could at the modular layout gatherings, and in between those times, your module would be part of a home layout. The rest of the trackwork could be a branch line (like the Ma & Pa?) served by your modern main line.

There are enough possible ways to compromise your dreams with reality to allow you to have the kind of model railroad you want in the space you have. You just have to be clever enough to discover which of those compro-

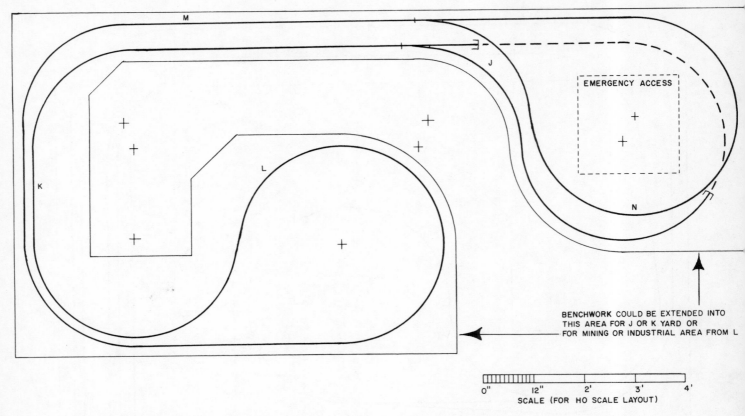

M

J

EMERGENCY ACCESS

K

L

N

BENCHWORK COULD BE EXTENDED INTO
THIS AREA FOR J OR K YARD OR
FOR MINING OR INDUSTRIAL AREA FROM L

0"   12"   2'   3'   4'
SCALE (FOR HO SCALE LAYOUT)

Fig. 12-8   BASIC LAYOUT IV: an HO scale loop-to-loop walk-around layout for a 7 x 14½-foot area.

mises will result in your getting what you want most. If you're not sure, then spend a few more months reading some books and magazines that deal with the kinds of real railroads you would consider as alternatives, and take another look at N scale, at modular model railroading and at the various narrow-gauge railroads to see if they might not be better suited to your needs. The object of this hobby is to bring that dream to life, even if you have to change some of the ''characters'' that make it live as only your railroad can.

There are still some pockets of history in America that continue to function the way everything did in the good old days. Modern technology and efficiency are, of course, available to everyone, but the initial costs are high indeed, as anyone who has been around for a new computer installation knows. There are places where the higher labor and maintenance costs of yesterday are lower than the costs of going modern. If you wander around the rural areas long enough, you'll still find sawmills where logs are carried in by railroads rather than trucks, machine shops powered by overhead belts rather than individual electric motors, and even a few short-line railroads.

The short line was part of America's growing-up period, the only link that communities had to the main-line railroads that in turn connected the major cities of the land. The automobile and the truck and their paved highways changed all that and made most short lines obsolete by the thirties. There are a large number of branch lines from the major railroads that fall into that same short-line category, and they too are vanishing one by one.

The short line is real railroading on a smaller scale. The short line may have just one locomotive or it may have twenty. Its major terminals and its train lengths are on the small time and small town scale. They're virtually models of the major lines, and that puts them closer to our miniature railroads. There's just no way to reduce Grand Central Station to fit even a club-size layout, but the complete roundhouses from Colorado City or Baltimore will fit nicely on many home-size model railroads.

If you're still searching for a prototype for your model railroad, let me recommend that you buy the book *The Ma & Pa* by George Hilton, published by Howell North. Some of the real railroad books are $40 and more, but this gem is less than $7 and includes maps of the trackage at the York and Baltimore yards as well as plans for the line's 0-6-0, 4-4-0, 4-6-0 and two 2-8-0 locomotives and for its gas-electric rail car, as well as photos of most of the stations and cabooses. The story of the

Modeling the Ma & Pa

Maryland & Pennsylvania's growth is very much like that of any short line, but the Ma & Pa has some delightful characteristics that make it seem almost like a story created by a model railroader. The railroad had some of the most picturesque and typically railroad locomotives, rolling stock and stations you could imagine; it connects with the popular Pennsylvania and the Baltimore & Ohio railroads, and its right of way is mostly that of some previous 3-foot narrow-gauge roads. It's the kind of a story that makes you want to apply it to other real railroads that weren't quite such perfect models, and I'd suggest you do just that.

I have attempted to capture the character of the Ma & Pa in a space that's enough smaller than a two-car garage to leave room for a workshop and laundry area (or, if the York shelf is eliminated, to fill a one-car garage) with HO scale models. I have included a double-track main line with broad curves on a level nearer the river bottoms to contrast with the tighter curves and climbing route of the Ma & Pa. The real Ma & Pa had almost as

Fig. 13-1   The south side of the North Avenue bridge in Baltimore with the original two-level station just visible over the top of the bridge and American (4-4-0) number 6 about to depart with a fan trip special over the Maryland & Pennsylvania. (*Photo from the J. E. Murphy collection, circa 1934.*)

many curves as a model railroad—it just didn't have as many right-hand ones. I'd make the double-track line the Baltimore & Ohio, but it could just as well be the Pennsy, and I'd operate it with some scheduled freight and passenger trains and an occasional peddler freight to switch the mine at Sewell and Whitemarsh. This double-track system adds some real complications to the layout, but it will keep you from ever becoming bored with the limitations of short-line railroading. There are some other advantages as well: the sight of two main-line trains—one eastbound and one westbound—circulating around that sweeping curve and down the riverbank will astonish your visitors when you add the actions of a third Ma & Pa train ambling around the hills to the scene. It will also impress you!

I have included a few extra switches so the trains on the main line can be reversed and so

at least three of them can be stored on hidden sidings so you don't always see the same two trains. The plan also has the switches needed so you can include a trip over the main line in each direction as part of a "long" route from York to Baltimore (see Figure 13-5) that is an HO scale 3.7 miles long. The strictly single-track run on the "pure" Ma & Pa trackage is about a mile and a half.

There is also the option of running the layout as an out-and-back plan to and from Baltimore for three reasons: to allow the layout to fit in a one-car garage; so you can build the layout in stages beginning with the double-track and ending with York; and so you have the delightful option of making the Ma & Pa trackage from Rocks to York narrow gauge or even dual narrow and standard gauge. The Ma & Pa could then be three railroads in one: a double-track main line, a

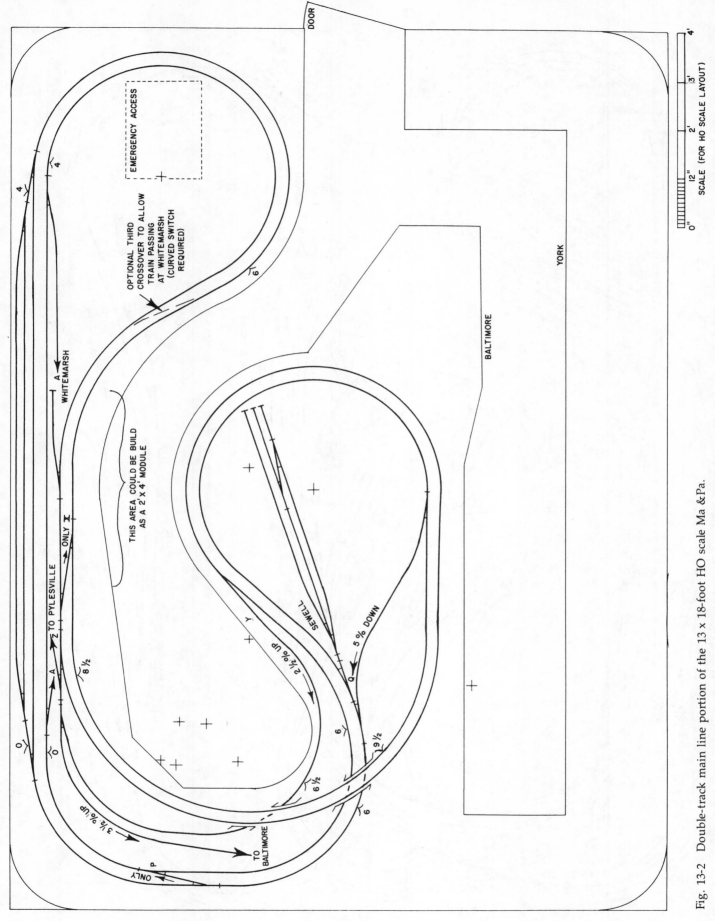

Fig. 13-2 Double-track main line portion of the 13 x 18-foot HO scale Ma &Pa.

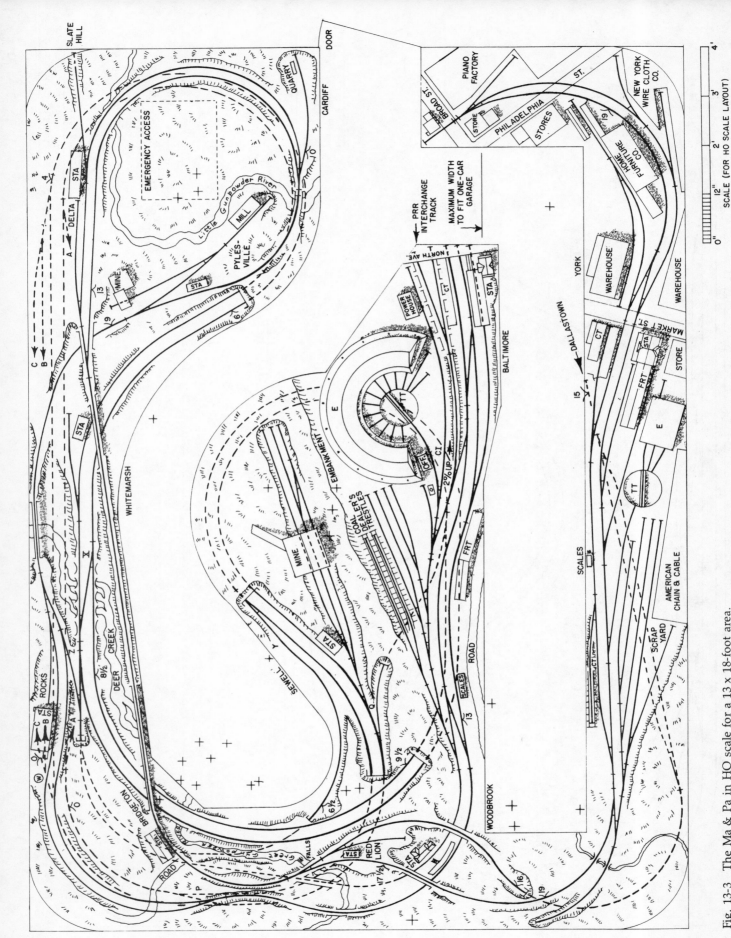

Fig. 13-3 The Ma & Pa in HO scale for a 13 x 18-foot area.

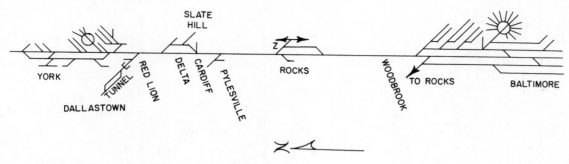

Fig. 13-4 Schematic of the short route from Baltimore to York.

standard gauge short line (the Maryland & Pennsylvania or almost any other) from Baltimore to Delta, and a narrow-gauge line from York to Rocks. Rocks could be enlarged slightly to serve as a narrow-to-standard gauge interchange point. I have incorporated the major features of both York and Baltimore using some selective compression; if you simply change the plan slightly in the area of those two towns, the Ma & Pa would work just as well for the combinations of railroads shown here.

Double Track Mainline RR	*Short Line RR*	*Narrow Gauge RR*
Baltimore & Ohio	Maryland & Pennsylvania	none
Western Pacific	Virginia & Truckee	Carson & Colo. (SP)
Pennsylvania	Shawmut (PS&N)	Big Level & Kinzua
Southern	Southern	Tweetsie (ET&WNC)
New York Central	New York Ontario & Western	none
Santa Fe	Colorado & Southern	Colorado & Southern
Rio Grande	Rio Grande	Rio Grande
New Haven	Boston & Maine	none
Boston & Albany	Maine Central	Sandy River (2-foot)
Southern Pacific	Southern Pacific	South Pacific Coast
Santa Fe	Sierra	Westside Lumber
Great Northern	Washington, Idaho & Montana	none
Northern Pacific (or UP)	Camas Prairie	none

The list could go on, of course. There are excellent hardback books on most of these railroads, as well as articles with track plans in back issues of the model railroad magazines that can help you to select the towns on each of them to substitute for places like York, Rocks, Delta, Baltimore, Sewell and Whitemarsh on the track plan. You can even pick your favorite prototypes and apply the Maryland & Pennsylvania's history to them or to a railroad of your own creation.

I must recommend that you eliminate the double-track portion of the track plan. That trackage adds too much complication to the benchwork and subbase, particularly near Red Lion and Delta. The double track does allow you to have just about every type of real railroading you could desire in a two-car garage or less, but it's a layout that should take at least 10 years to even begin to reach completion. It is drawn so you can choose just the double-track portion (Figure 13-2) and it's a matter of eliminating the few tracks that connect with the double track to model just the Maryland & Pennsylvania portion. It should be easy enough to imagine how simple and enjoyable a railroad this would be with just that single-track railroad. I would keep the hidden track route from Woodbrook to Delta to serve as a hidden storage track and

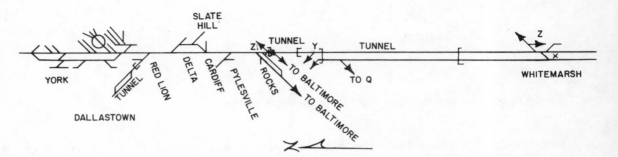

Fig. 13-5   Schematic of the long route from Baltimore to York.

a source of interchange traffic. If the Baltimore peninsula is reduced to the width of the Ma & Pa trackwork, then the layout is even better suited to walk-around control, because the engineers don't have to move around the peninsula when their trains move from Woodbrook to Rocks. Alternatively, you could continue the track at Red Lion to where Sewell is located and loop it below Baltimore and back to the vicinity of Red Lion to save the wasted "walk" when trains travel between York and Red Lion. The layout is designed for walk-around control, but the Baltimore peninsula does present those problems.

FIDDLE YARDS AND INTERCHANGES

If I were to build the Ma & Pa layout in Figure 13-3, I would try to muster enough courage to eliminate the Baltimore yard even if it meant moving it to where York is and reversing the order of the towns so there was no York on the layout. I would then fill that Baltimore area with some countryside and perhaps a town called Red Lion on one side of the peninsula and a visible branch line to Dallastown on the opposite side. I have included both yards for the same reasons I've included a double-track main line; to show you what is possible, because the dream is sometimes more important to follow through on paper to save overdoing it in the reality of

Fig. 13-6   The Ma & Pa's two-level Baltimore station taken from the railroad side with the shed over the two passenger tracks in the foreground. (*Photo from the J. E. Murphy collection.*)

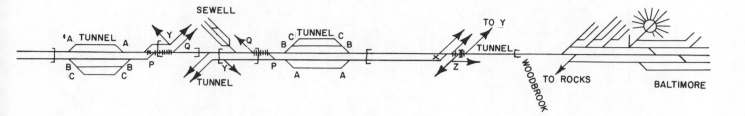

HHHH CROSSED LINES INDICATE ONLY TRACKS
TRAVELED OVER TWICE ON LONG
ROUTE FROM BALTIMORE TO YORK

the actual model railroad. York or Baltimore—depending on which one you feel you could do without—would then be nothing more than a hidden reversing loop in about the same location and level as Sewell. One yard is more than enough for any model railroad. The track plan might appear to be a self-contained railroad that merely hauls whatever York needs from Baltimore or vice versa. The

yards are deceiving here, because they do not appear to extend beyond the layout, but on the prototype they do indeed, and I would recommend that you operate the railroad that way.

The real Maryland & Pennsylvania is one of those bridge railroads that might be used when the quickest railroad route to or from Baltimore was through York. The Ma & Pa's

Fig. 13-7   The three-stall engine house and turntable at York in 1972.

Fig. 13-8 The Delta station prior to restoration. It has since been repainted and re-stored to an 1890 appearance. (*Photo from the I. E. Murphy collection.*)

Fig. 13-9 The Whiteford, Maryland, station now has its windows boarded over. Note the grain elevator in the background. (*Photo from the J. E. Murphy collection.*)

Fig. 13-10 The York station, office and freight house in 1972.

Fig. 13-11 The double-track portion of the miniature Ma & Pa layout should be detailed with scenery and one tunnel portal to match this 1950-era scene near Clarksburg, West Virginia, on the premerger Baltimore & Ohio. (*Photo courtesy the Chessie system.*)

Fig. 13-12 A portion of the eastern-style stone arch bridges, like this one near Harrisburg, Pennsylvania, should be included on the double-track portion of the Ma & Pa layout. This is the famed Broadway Limited in about 1939 with a streamlined K-4 Pacific (4-6-2) pulling a train of heavyweight steel cars.

tracks connect directly with the Pennsylvania at Baltimore, and at York, and with the Baltimore & Ohio at Baltimore—that's where most of the Ma & Pa's freight traffic travels in both directions. The stub end of the railroad across Broad Street in York (in Figure 13-3) would be a perfect place for one of those combination road-crossing car-rerailers that come in most train sets. All of the cars to and from the Pennsylvania could then be moved on and off the layout by hand—a similar PRR interchange track is located beneath the North Avenue bridge in Baltimore.

If you would rather have the bulk of the railroad's traffic appear and disappear under its own power, use the hidden route from Woodbrook to Rocks (the place where I have located the Baltimore & Ohio interchange with the actual double-track B & O) and/or the hidden track from Red Lion to Dallastown.

Dallastown was really a dead-end branch line, but there's no reason why you couldn't use it as the interchange with the Pennsy or some other connecting line—I would, and that's why the Dallastown tracks are so close to the edge of the table—interchange cars can be taken on and off the layout at Dallastown and the locomotives can even run around their trains to reappear at Red Lion for travel in either direction. When you use a hidden yard for such a purpose, it's generally referred to as a fiddle yard because it's the only place where you are "fiddling" with the pure-scale reality of your model railroad empire. The three passing sidings at AA, BB and CC could be used as a fiddle yard as well, but they are somewhat inaccessible. Those three tracks are there to allow you to vary the traffic on the double-track main line as much as possible by holding trains on those sidings.

Structures and Scenery

The term *realistic* is far more difficult to put into practice than it is to define. The definition is simple enough; if your models look like the real thing, then they're realistic. The difficulty lies in truly seeing what the real thing looks like. There is no kit made that will be realistic when you take it from the box or even when you've painted it and added decals. The prototype for that model lives in a real world that literally colors it with what is called weathering in Chapter III. That simple touch with an airbrush and some thinned-down paint will make most locomotives and rolling stock models as realistic as they can be.

Structures too should be weathered in the same way, but it takes a bit more to make a structure look real, because the environment surrounding the building is almost as important as the building itself when it comes to capturing the feeling of realism. Part of that feeling is created by the fact that no two buildings are ever alike. Weathering can make all the difference that's needed between two models of the same freight cars or locomotives (with number changes, of course), but there must be some major changes in the colors, the surroundings and even in the shapes of structure models for them to be as realistic as a well-weathered locomotive or freight car.

THE INDIVIDUAL

You are the one who is the most important when it comes time to decide whom to please with your model railroad. Your family and friends are probably the next on that list of those you hope will share your appreciation for your models. Most of us consider fellow model railroaders, though, to be the critics whose opinions—whether we like to admit it or not—we value second only to our own. Of course most of us are critics too when we look at photographs of others' work in books and magazines and decide whether or not we consider that scene realistic. The photographer plays a most important part in those judgments, and it's a good idea to remind yourself

XIV
Structure Conversions

that some very good modeling ideas are still visible in some of those most-unrealistic or blurred photographs.

One of the pitfalls in your path toward creating truly realistic structures is the very existence of all those other railroads and their builders and those photographers who take their pictures. They buy the same structure kits that you do, and no matter how they place them on their layouts or what colors they paint them, their buildings look just like yours if both came from the same kit. There are hundreds of building kits on the market, and most of them are recognizable because hundreds of photographs of them have appeared in print.

The problem is especially noticeable with the inexpensive and easy-to-assemble plastic kits—those models are popular with model railroaders, too popular to be realistic. The craftsman kits like Campbell's, SS Limited's, Fine Scale's, Dyna-Model's and the like are sold in fewer quantities, but most of those structures are of such fascinating prototypes that you will recognize them on any layout

135

Fig. 14-1   The houses and mine in this N scale scene are Faller's European prototype plastic kits with some of the fancy trim removed and weathering added to give them an American appearance.

Fig. 14-2   Early-era structures are often the scenic background for locomotive shots. The Winton & Co. and its neighboring industries, photographed on the Erie Railroad at Port Jervis, New York, circa 1915, would make fine structures for any model railroad. (*Photo from the Harold K. Vollrath collection.*)

after having seen even a photo of them just once. The problem is unique to structures, because you don't expect to see more than one Bertha's Brewery, but you do expect to see hundreds or even thousands of almost-identical Santa Fe boxcars, and the recent pooling of diesel power makes the sight of a Southern Pacific diesel in New York no great shock. You do not, however, expect to see the same structures in California that you would in New York, even if they are something as standard as a railroad handcar house.

It's ironic, in a way, that model railroaders tend to buy as many different freight cars as they can when purchases of lots of four or more identical cars would be more like the prototype. For some reason, we tend to want the same structures that appear on other model railroads. Part of the reason is price, another is availability, and a third may be that the creation of a complete model railroad taxes our imaginations to the point where we would just rather not worry about the buildings.

Another irony of the proliferation of identical model structures is that almost all of them have been assembled from kits that could almost as easily have been modified, during assembly, as built box-stock. Structure kits, even the plastic ones, have their walls and roofs as separate pieces that can be easily cut or altered before the kit is completed so the finished structure will be different from any other. The process of making one or more model kits into something different than what is illustrated on the box top is called cross-kitting or converting or kit-bashing. It works just as well with locomotives or freight cars or passenger cars as it does with buildings, but it's a whole lot easier with buildings.

CONVERSIONS

Structure conversions will generally only require one more tool than those needed to build the building stock; an X-Acto razor saw blade number 235 with a number 5 handle is less than $4, and it can be used for other modeling work including cutting insulating gaps in track rails. You'll also need a steel ruler or straight-edge, a hobby knife and white glue (for wood kits), ACC or cyanoacrylate cement (for metal or wood-and-metal kits) or liquid (not tube-type) cement for plastic kits. A small woodworker's or machinist's square is also helpful but not essential. If you are working with plastic models, a medium-cut metal file can make fitting some of the joints much faster than using sandpaper or shaving the parts with a knife. The number 200 and 400 grits of wet or dry sandpaper can be useful too, for obtaining precise fits between cut parts.

There is one other "tool" that you'll need to

Fig. 14-3 Rub light grey mortar-colored paint over plastic brick sheets or the sides of brick building kits so the grey fills in just the crevices.

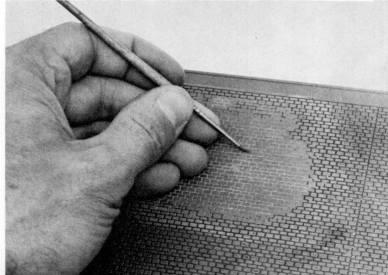

Fig. 14-4 Use a number 0-size brush to touch about every twentieth brick with a lighter or darker shade for the random coloring effect of real brickwork.

Fig. 14-5 Decals or dry transfers will help to highlight the texture of the brickwork.

make your buildings as realistic as your trains—imagination. Try to rearrange your thinking to "see" any structure kit as just a box of parts rather than as a complete building. If you can do that, you're well on your way to completing the creation by arranging those parts into some different shapes. One of the easiest things to imagine is a doubling of the length of the structure, which is necessary to get most engine-house kits to fit the locomotives you expect them to. Go on from there and envision what the kit might look like

Fig. 14-6 Wrap the base of the structure in Saran Wrap and brush plaster and "dirt" around it to give the effect that the building is sitting in the ground.

with two or three stories or, if it's a two-story building already, what it would look like as a single-story structure.

It usually takes two kits to make a conversion, because you'll find you want a bit more than one kit includes to make, for example, those two-story conversions. With two kits, you can assemble a building using only the long walls from both kits or only the short walls. That razor saw will be necessary to trim the ends of the parts so they can be fitted together in a manner other than that intended by the kit manufacturer. Don't be afraid to use the windows or doors from one kit in another, or to buy the extra door and window castings sold by Grandt, Campbell, Timberline, MDC and others. It's easy enough to file the openings in the thin wood or plastic walls a bit larger to install new windows or doors. The leftover parts from the kits can serve as your own "lumberyard" full of doors, windows, chimneys, walls and roofs for other conversions, or to use in building smaller structures like handcar houses.

The general practices of the prototype are just as important when you're building a structure as they are with locomotives and cars. You can freelance your structures to some extent, but pay particular attention to any changes you might have to make in the slope or pitch of the roofs, and be sure to include plenty of overhang, even it means making a complete new roof. Sheets of plastic roof material are sold by Vollmer, and Campbell's paper shingles are available in most hobby shops. Cardboard or .030-inch thick styrene sheet can be used for the roof with Campbell's shingles or strips of black construction paper to simulate tar paper for the surface.

If you've made a major change in the kit, be sure to add a few interior braces for strength. Slip some cardboard walls inside any building to prevent the viewer from looking into one window and out the other for that vacant appearance. Don't forget to build some type of foundation that is set into the scenery, to set the structure itself into the scenery, or to build a platform around the structure so it looks as if it actually is attached to the ground in some way.

Fig. 14-7 The small details are the essential elements of any realistic scene. Gordon Johnson's abandoned farmhouse (left, rear) is a national contest winner, and his pair of "lived-in" houses are just as realistic.

Fig. 14-8 The two houses were scratch-built using commercial strip wood and plastic brick sheets. The tree is picture-hanging wire covered with epoxy.

Fig. 14-9 Would you remember to have gopher holes, a swing with a broken rope, a barrel with trash in it or sunflowers on your layout? Those are the details that make the buildings look alive.

Fig. 14-10 The two Johnson houses are built in HO scale on a 1-foot square board. It's easier to add details around a building when its base can be moved to the work-bench.

The bridges can be one of the real pitfalls of model railroading and there's no pun intended. There's a basic difference in the design parameters that we have for our bridges as compared to those of the real railroads. The real railroads only build a bridge whenever they must, while model railroaders do the best they can to design a layout that will use as many bridges as possible. Once again, there's only one way to create a credible scene, and that's to study the prototype to see how they fit their bridges into the scenery. You'll be working backwards because you'll be fitting your scenery to the bridges, but there's not much you can do about that. If you have selected some particular prototype for your model railroad, then you're well ahead of the game because you can copy both that road's scenery and its bridges. Try to avoid buying a bridge because you like it and then having to find some way to fit it into your layout. It's much better to find a photograph of a real railroad bridge that you like, and then locate a model to match it.

Bridges

SELECTIVE COMPRESSION

The real railroad bridges will almost always be longer than those you want for your railroad. For one thing, the hills are higher on those real railroads than they are on most model railroads and the valleys are deeper, so there's more to bridge. The Spokane International, for instance, uses a total of five Howe truss bridges in Bonners Ferry, Idaho. Each one of these bridges is about half again as long as the one in Campbell's HO scale kit, so a model of that set of spans in HO scale would be a whopping 8 feet long. There isn't room on most model railroads for prototype-length bridges and the railroad too, unless those bridges are reduced in length a bit. The Campbell HO scale Howe truss bridge captures the spirit of the Spokane International's bridges by having true-to-scale width, height and timber dimensions but less length. Three of Campbell's bridges would only run about 3½ feet, and you'd still capture all of the feeling of the real thing. The principle of reducing only one or two of the major overall dimensions is called selective compression.

There were hundreds of wood Howe truss bridges and wooden trestles on American railroads during the steam era. Only a few of them survive, thanks in part to the sparks from those steam locomotives we miss so much. Most of those wooden Howe truss bridges—there are also steel Howe trusses—were built with wooden bridge piers and a wood trestle at each end. A more modern bridge would have an earthen fill at each end with concrete bridge piers. There was no standard length to a Howe truss, but those on the Spokane International were about as long as was practical. If the span was only equal to four bays of the Howe, then a straining beam or through timber bridge like the one on the Rio Grande (and Campbell's HO scale kit number 762) was used. A modern replacement would be a through plate girder bridge like Tyco's HO scale plastic model. You can find examples of the modern steel and concrete bridges just by driving along any railroad. Most of the brick and stone bridges

Fig. 15-1   It's a rare sight indeed to find wooden bridges still standing as reminders of the exciting age of the steam locomotive.

Fig. 15-2 This curved wood trestle was assembled from bass wood strips by Lonnie Shay for his HOn3 layout.

are still standing on the eastern railroads. The wooden bridge, though, is becoming as rare as a wooden freight car.

The wooden trestle was once the most common bridge design on the full-size railroads. Its major shortcoming was that, like all wood bridges, it was susceptible to fires, and fires were carried in every steam locomotive's firebox with the sparks that flew out of every smokestack. One of the essential details of any wooden bridge is the little platforms that hold the barrels of water or sand that were used to stop fires. The brakeman and conductor were supposed to take a hard look rearward after their train passed over any wooden bridge so they could stop the train or at least telegraph the news of a bridge fire.

Most wooden trestles were not replaced by bridges at all, they were simply buried in dirt dumped between and beside the ties. If there was a small stream at the base of the trestle bents, a culvert of concrete or corrugated steel was constructed just before the dirt-dumping

operations began. The long wooden trestle is a sight that most model railroaders try to include on a layout of any size and for very good reasons. You're missing a rare chance at some even more realistic prototype details if you don't build a long fill or embankment with the tracks on top and a culvert below.

Fig. 15-3 The NWSL Chopper (shown) and the Shay Wood Miter are tools that make strip wood cutting much easier and far more accurate.

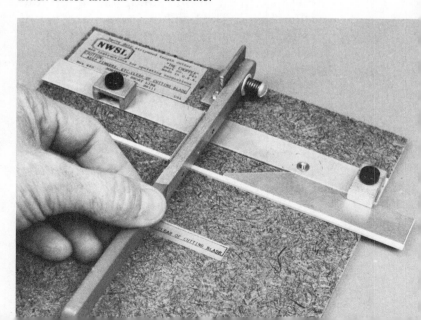

Fig. 15-4   Larry Nyce used strip wood with Grandt nut-bolt-washer castings to create the replica of one of the trestles on the Rio Grande Southern's now abandoned narrow-guage line.

You can tell your visitors that it's really a model of a buried trestle. Those long fills are far more common on real railroads than trestles, but they're seldom seen on a model railroad.

The National Model Railroad Association's DATA PAK book is $10 to members, and it's money well worth spending to obtain some otherwise hard-to-find information on the real railroads. The book includes a number of essential modeling measurements and data as well. The NMRA book illustrates how and where the various types of real railroad bridges were used. With that information you can scratch-build your own bridges from the scale lumber bass wood strips sold by Camino and Northeastern, or combine several kits to duplicate the practices of the prototype railroads. The timber trestles and timber Howe and through trusses are fairly complex structures when completed, but they're

made up from fairly simple "units" that can be assembled over full-scale patterns. Buy at least one of the Campbell HO or N scale kits before you decide it would be easier or cheaper to make your own. In many cases it's less expensive to combine several kits for a larger bridge than it is to buy the basic materials.

The various types of steel truss bridges are hard to find as kits in any scale. There are several different European-made plastic kits for steel versions of the wooden Howe truss, but most of them are enough different from American railroad practice to look a bit strange. The NMRA book will give you some examples of typical American steel bridges (there are many others), but your only safe bet is to find a real bridge or a picture of one to duplicate. You can often use the parts from those plastic bridge kits with some of the conversion or cross-kitting techniques to make

Fig. 15-5 The open-top wood truss bridges are generally called straining beam truss bridges. This one is on the still-operating Denver and Rio Grande narrow-guage line north of Durango, Colorado.

Fig. 15-6 These wood truss bridges are generally called Howe trusses.

Fig. 15-7 Five of the relics of the steam age still survive to carry the trains of the Spokane International Railroad near Bonners Ferry, Idaho.

almost perfect replicas of American bridges. One of the most common mistakes a modeler will make, when selecting a "steel" bridge, is to pick one of the Howe-type bridges to span an area that the prototype would have used a simple culvert or at best a short deck or through steel girder bridge to cover. The big bridges over the tracks on the prototype are almost always long bridges as well. Most of those plastic kits can be made into more realistic models by combining two kits to build a bridge that's half-again as long as the kit or longer.

BUILDING UP TO A BRIDGE

Real railroad practices should always be your guide for a model railroad. That is particularly important when it comes to bridges, because a badly placed bridge can do more than any other effect to make your railroad look like a toy. The real railroads use their bridges as a last resort for spanning a gap. Model railroaders too often try to reverse that concept by having too much bridge and too little scenery. Start observing the prototype railroads to see just how they use their bridges. You won't find a whole lot of bridges, but you will find hundreds of small concrete or steel culverts. A model railroader would probably have put a long steel truss or deck girder bridge in those same situations.

Fig. 15-8 The nut-bolt-washer castings, wire rods and a spike set in every tie helped make Joseph Kolsis's Howe truss a contest winner.

Fig. 15-9 A snow shed built during the wood bridge era was built very much like a bridge. This one was built by the Central Pacific (now the Southern Pacific) in 1867 near the summit of Donner Pass, California. (*Photo courtesy of the Southern Pacific Railroad.*)

When you're planning your layout, leave plenty of places for those earth fills and culverts. When you build the benchwork, cut the subbase and Homosote roadbed close enough to the ties so you can have plenty of places for fills, and, when there's place for a cut, the drainage ditches beside the tracks. A real railroad will usually use an earth fill to a height of at least 10 feet before they install a wood trestle's first bents. If there's a bridge with a concrete abutment, that abutment is usually backed with an earthen fill that's 20 feet high or more and probably 20 yards long. Those sections of fill are as important as the bridges in capturing the feeling of the real railroads.

Lightweight Scenery

You'd think that a model railroader would be satisfied to make rocks and dirt that looked like rocks and dirt. Making such scenic effects lightweight seems to be asking too much. If you know you've moved into your last home and that your layout will never again have to be moved, then you don't need to worry about what your scenery weighs. If you're building one of the modular layouts, though, you'll curse every extra ounce when it's time to move the module to one of the club layout collections for a weekend's operation with other modules. That's the time when you'll want to join me in the search for the feather-weight rocks. There are some real volcanic stones that weigh about 10 percent of what they appear to weigh, but they are far too porous for a model railroad. If you want light-weight rocks, you'll have to make your own.

There are two basic methods of producing lightweight scenery; make it from very thin and strong plaster like Hydrocal and watch the amount of wood bracing and plaster rock castings you use, or make your scenery from plastic. Some of us have trouble justifying to

148

ourselves the use of plastic for any model, and the thought of making dirt and rocks from the stuff is too much to comprehend. If you're one of those, let me suggest that you find a lumberyard that has some Hydrocal-brand plaster. You will also need some industrial-grade paper towels or a lot of old sheets and tee shirts. The basic scenery shapes will be formed with those Hydrocal-soaked paper towels or rags. The rags, especially if they're sheets, are a bit better and stronger, so you might get by with less plaster and hence less weight. There's no substitute for that Hydrocal, however.

PAPER-THIN PLASTER

The basic shapes for the mountains and valleys can be built up with wadded newspapers, empty corrugated cartons or even pillows. When the Hydrocal sets, those props can be removed so the plaster will be self-supporting. You will need to cut some pieces of ¼-inch plywood or masonite for the front or rear edges of the table to support the peaks of the hills and mountains. One layer of Hydrocal-soaked paper towels or rags will be strong enough to be self-supporting over a 6-inch span; larger areas will need at least two layers. Use enough Hydrocal to hide the grain of the paper towels and the weave of the cloth. You can help by brushing over the surface with your hands during the setting stages; the hardened portions of the Hydrocal plaster will break off and roughen the texture to look like dirt. If you're modeling just dirt-covered (or grass-covered) gentle slopes, that's all the plaster you'll need—the next stage will be to sift actual dirt and flocking over the terrain. Precolor the Hydrocal by mixing some dry colors for plaster walls in with the plaster powder and water. It will be easier to color the "earth" later, and if you do happen to chip the Hydrocal or miss coloring an area, there won't be that awful white plaster showing through.

The techniques of casting rocks in latex rubber molds can be modified slightly for lighter-weight scenery. Add the "rocks" as

Fig. 16-1 When your model railroad is a portable module or diorama, you have to find some ways to make those rocks weigh less than they appear to. This is part of Larry Nyce's HOn3 diorama.

part of that second layer of paper towels or cloth-soaked Hydrocal. Make a few latex and cloth molds from liquid latex (Mountains-in-Minutes sells it and so do most craft supply shops) and gauze or muslin as shown in the photos. Vary the texture of the molds by using two or three different types of real rocks for the patterns with at least one mold made over a piece of coal. When you're ready for that second layer of Hydrocal, spray the first layer with water in the areas where you'll add rocks. Cut the sheets or tear the paper towels into squares of about 6 inches or less. Pour about ¼-inch of the Hydrocal, water and dry coloring mix into the latex mold. Soak one or two pieces of paper towel or rag in the mixture, push it into the latex mold, and spread the cloth or paper towel out in the mold. The whole gooey mess can now be slapped

against the prewetted Hydrocal "mountain" and held there for the moment or two it takes for the Hydrocal to set. The latex rubber should be flexible enough to conform to the shape of the mountain while giving the real rock's texture to the surface.

When the Hydrocal has just set, peel the latex mold away. You'll have to repeat the process several times to finish a small area of rock texture, mixing fresh batches of Hydrocal, water and dry coloring each time. With some practice you can keep the actual plaster thickness down to a quarter-inch or less. Be sure to leave some roughened Hydrocal surfaces (added as a second layer) on the tops of hills and in the valleys as "dirt" to contrast with the rock textures. Finally, stain the rocks with diluted Rit dye, and add the loose dirt to the horizontal faces.

Fig. 16-2 Two layers of paper towels soaked in Hydrocal are strong enough to be self-supporting scenery. Be sure to include the drainage ditches on the uphill side of the tracks.

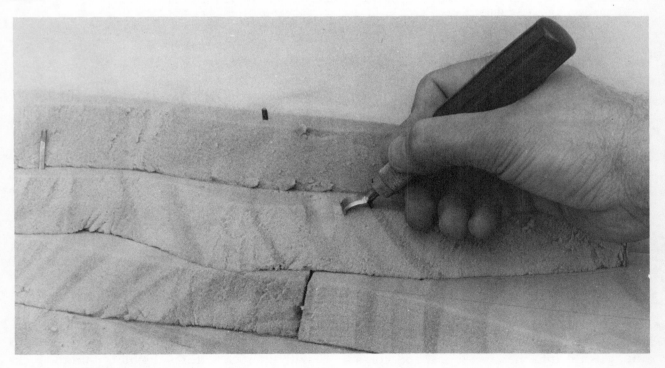

Fig. 16-3 The lightweight urethane foam used for insulation can be cut (with a jigsaw and very little effort) into contour blocks and then shaped with an X-Acto wood chisel.

Fig. 16-4 The back side of a typical hill and tunnel showing the layers of foam plastic, the latex paint thickened with sawdust and the final ground cover of lichen and glued-on sawdust.

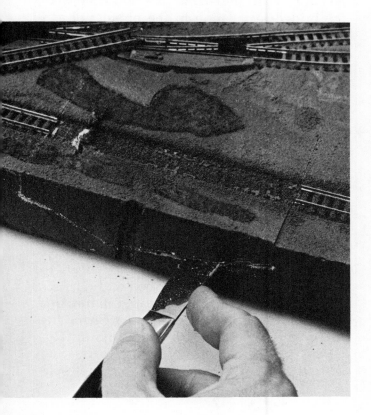

PLASTIC ROCKS

There are two types of hard foam plastic that can be used to create ultra-lightweight scenery. You can use the 2-inch thick sheets of expanded polyfoam to build up the mountains, or you can use the Mountains-in-Minutes kits to mix your own expanded polyfoam and brush it over wadded paper hills or mold it in latex molds. The end product, in either case, will be that fine-pore off-white plastic foam that looks like a hardened bathroom sponge. You'll have to search among the industrial packing firms to find the sheets of polyfoam, but most model railroad shops carry Mountains-in-Minutes products.

Fig. 16-5 The urethane foam can also be used as a tabletop for small HO layouts, N layouts and dioramas. If you want to add a river, simply cut the plastic with a steak knife.

Fig. 16-6 Smooth the surface of the shaped urethane with a wire brush before painting on thickened latex paint.

Fig. 16-8 Apply a layer of gauze or cheesecloth between each of three or four coats of liquid latex to give the finished mold more resistance to tearing.

Layouts up to about 2 x 4 feet can be made directly on sheets of polyfoam, but it's not something I would recommend for everyone. The polyfoam has virtually no holding strength for nails, and it's soft enough to shift even beneath a layer of glue, paint or plaster. It's almost impossible to have reliable and strong trackwork. I would suggest that you

Fig. 16-7 Brush liquid latex over a real rock or a piece of coal after the porous surface has been coated with mold release.

lay your track on a conventional plywood subbase with Homosote roadbed and open-grid type benchwork. The benchwork can be made of 1" x 2" boards set 18 inches apart for a portable layout, because the plastic scenery will be light enough not to require the usual heavy benchwork. When the trackwork is complete, the expanded polyfoam sheets can be cut to fit in the open areas and even, like the bridge installation in the photos, placed beneath the tracks where there will be bridges. The mountains can be hollow to save on the material. The polyfoam can be cut with a steak knife, but the larger contour-shaped panels should be cut with a small jigsaw. The Dremel-brand Moto-Shop electric jigsaw is perfect for this type of work.

The Mountains-in-Minutes scenery kits contain the two-part polyfoam plastic and catalyst liquids with full instructions on how to mix and use them. The liquids expand to about 30 times their fluid volume, so a little goes a long way. There are two ways to use these liquids: either apply them over the hills and valleys shaped from polyfoam sheets to make rocks like those described with Hydrocal, or just pour them over paper mountains and let them bubble and expand. Shape the mountains and valleys as you would for Hydrocal with wadded-up newspapers, and cover them with some slightly wet newspapers—they shape better that way—to give a smooth surface for the polyfoam. The polyfoam goes through a state in which it looks and acts much like shaving cream, and that's the time to slop it over those mountains. If you don't get the shapes you want, either add more polyfoam, or carve and shape it the same way that's shown for the sheets of polyfoam. Rocks, cast in latex molds from the same polyfoam liquids, can be attached to the hills wherever you wish.

The polyfoams carve quite easily, and they're soft enough so they can be smoothed by just brushing them with a wire brush. The plastic is messy, though, because it makes something like sawdust when you carve or saw or brush it. It's the kind of job that should be done outdoors on a calm day, because you may be allergic to that plastic dust. When you're through shaping mountains, seal all of the surfaces with a thick layer of latex wall paint, even the underside of the

Fig. 16-9 Fill the latex molds with precolored plaster, and just as the plaster begins to harden, slap the plaster-filled mold against the mountain and hold it there until the plaster finishes setting.

Fig. 16-10 Apply some darker brown or grey stain diluted in water to accent the cracks and fissures in the rock casting and finish the scene with some loose "dirt" glued to the horizontal faces.

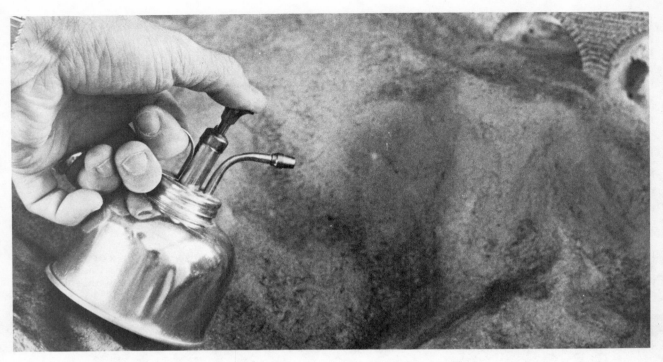

Fig. 16-11   The hand-pump type of brass atomizer intended for spraying plants is perfect for applying a mist of glue or water to a plaster hill to prepare it for surface textures.

Fig. 16-12   Buy one of the self-turning types of flour sieves to apply real dirt, sawdust, flocking or other surface textures.

Fig. 16-13 Fill the gaps between the track rails and spiked-down guard rails with thick string while you trowel-on the plaster road surface. Remove the string the moment the plaster begins to set.

scenery, to keep any additional dust particles from flaking off. If you need to glue the poly-foam, use white glue because most contact cements and plastic glues will melt the poly-foam. Finish the surface with the same dirt and grass textures you'd use over plaster, and you'll never know that those hills are plastic until it comes time to pick them up.

XVII
The River

There's really only one way to make water on a model railroad. There are a lot of variations on that theme, though, to make that "water" look like the real lakes, rivers, ponds, rapids and bubbling streams. Real water is far too thick for use on even an O scale model railroad. Take a close look at some of the special effects in those sea disaster films, and notice that the one flaw is that the water acts like glue. Alcohol is closer to what HO scale water might be like, but it's a dangerous substance to leave in the open even if you could figure some way to keep it from evaporating overnight. Fluids of any kind are far more trouble than their effect is worth on a model railroad, especially when there's something better. Clear epoxy casting resin is the best possible choice for any kind of water. It's the same material that is used, with fiberglass cloth, to repair boats and other fiberglass items, so try a boat-repair shop or a craft supply store. Try to find some of the green and blue and brown dyes the craft people use, and some of their pearl tints while you're shopping.

There are some pitfalls that you must be aware of when using casting resin to simulate water. Experiment on some imitation scenery made with the same materials you used for the good stuff to see how it reacts to the resin. The resin seems to grip a fairly rough surface better than it does a smooth one. There cannot be any trace of loose "dirt" or plaster dust or whatever in the bottom of the lake or river. If the casting resin fails to grip the bottom of the lake or river, small patches of what seem to be trapped bubbles will appear that detract from the realism. The best surface seems to be precolored Hydrocal that has been roughened while in the setting state. Some of the worst things for the bottoms are latex paint, smooth (as it dries) plaster or Hydrocal and dry plaster dust or real dirt. In other words, it's safest to pour the "water" for your layout before you apply the ground covering materials.

If you do have real dirt around your casting resin lakes or rivers, I would suggest you seal it with a good soaking of white glue and water. The casting resin flows like water, and it will turn dirt and some plasters a darker shade that looks like wet dirt or wet plaster, and that color will remain forever because the resin doesn't evaporate. Be particularly careful to seal every crack in the bottoms of lakes and streams. Even a pinhole seam between two of those Hydrocal-soaked paper towels or rags is enough to let the resin through. To be safe, put pans and papers below the lakes and streams until the casting resin sets.

The casting resin is a two-part substance with a resin and a catalyst. Mix the two precisely as outlined on the labels. Most casting resins set with the surface still slightly tacky. Craft stores sell clear paints to coat the surface and give it a hard and perfectly dry feeling. Most types of clear paint will work, but again try it on a scrap of sample scenery to be sure it doesn't crack or craze or even dissolve the resin. Clear Varathane-brand paint seems to be the best and dries with the least amount of yellowing. The Varathane can in fact be used by itself for very small ponds and streams.

The edges of casting resin "water" can be most disappointing because the meniscus of the resin flows up the banks for a most unreal-

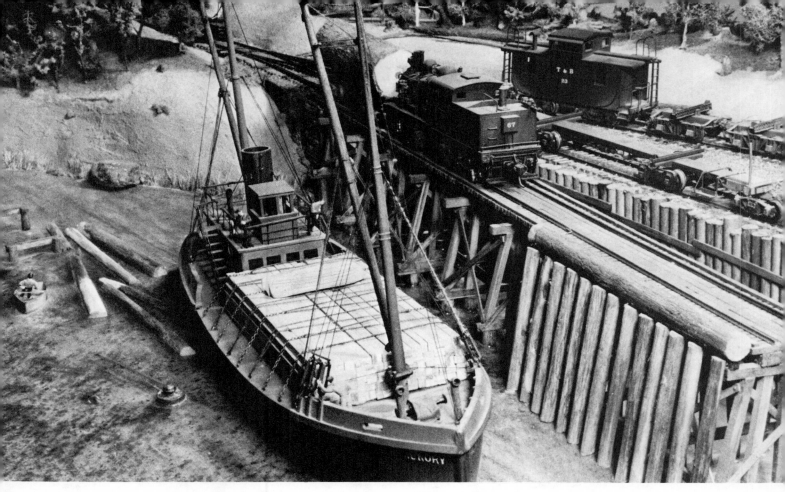

Fig. 17-1 Gordon Johnson added small drops of green stain to the still-wet middle layers of epoxy resin to create the algae effect of still water.

istic distance. The only answer to that problem is to paint the edges of the "water" with white glue and dust on some real dirt, grass or ground foam to form the edge of the water. Be careful about how much resin you pour at any one time. It might crack if the depth is more than about a half-inch. You will find that you don't need too much depth for a deep effect; just add a bit of blue or green dye to that first pouring, a bit less to the second pouring, and none at all for the last one or two. There should be no place on the layout where a river or lake deeper than 2 to 3 inches is necessary. Be sure to have any cut hemp or cattail "weeds" ready to place into the resin for the edges of the water or for any marsh areas.

Rushing streams, rapids and waterfalls are the most difficult types of water to model even with casting resin. Be wary of using real rocks for such streams, unless you wash them thoroughly in water to remove any traces of

the dust and dirt that form bubbles in the resin. It is far easier to make a resin stream if you can tilt the stream so it is level until the resin cures. That's often possible with a diorama or a module layout, but difficult with an around-the-wall model railroad. An alternative method is to brush the casting resin into the stream or river just before it begins to cure. The resin goes through a very brief state when it gets tacky and then gelatinlike just before it hardens. This only lasts for a minute or two, so you can work with only a foot or so of the stream at a time. Be cautious and work outdoors, because the casting resin gives off its nastiest vapors as it is curing. Some of the craft stores have a type of retarder for the resin that holds in that gelatinlike state for as much as 15 minutes. You must experiment with it, however, to determine how much does the kind of job you need. Remember that resin flows like water; it just moves a lot slower. Don't be fooled into thinking you've

Fig. 17-2   A sunken rowboat, scraps of wood and shoreline weeds all help to convey the impression of real water on Gordon Johnson's layout.

Fig. 17-3   Al Love used clear casting resin for the small stream on his HO scale diorama with finely sifted dirt for the earth.

Fig. 17-4 Frank Barone powders real granite for his earth. The real dirt will soak up some of the first pouring of epoxy resin, so plan on filling most areas with two or more batches of the resin.

made an uphill puddle and walk away, because that puddle will have flowed on "downstream" the next time you look.

The most effective way of bringing water to the edge of the layout is to make a profile of the bottom of the stream, using Masonite or plywood for the contoured-to-match table edge. Buy some of that grey plastic air-conditioning duct tape and use it to build a dam across the edge of the table that is higher than the greatest depth of the lake or river you are pouring. When the resin cures, the tape dam can be removed, and you get an aquariumlike effect of being able to see into the water's edge. If the area near the tape is large, reinforce the tape with a piece of plywood temporarily nailed to the table edge. If you are going to have some fairly large ships in your casting resin lake or harbor, the effect will be more realistic if you remove a section of the bottom of the ship, so no more than 2 inches of it need be submerged in the resin to bring the

resin up to the ship's waterline. The murky effect of the blue or green dye and the refraction effect will hide the missing keel area of the ship.

There are several ways to produce an effective white-water effect with casting resin. You will want to use the almost-cured gelatinlike tricks to get the resin into the river or stream. When it's there, keep picking at it with the tip of a knife right up to the time when it completely cures to its hardest state. The last few "picks" will actually produce little scraps and chunks of the resin. Brush over those with a second coating of the resin to give them that wet look, and at the same time, dab some white dye and a trace of pearl dye into the area. It only takes a touch (even a drop is too much) of the white or pearl dye to give the white-water effect—if you went too far, try brushing yet another layer of resin over the area, but with some blue or green dye mixed in to tone down the white or pearl.

Fig. 17-5 The epoxy resin in this steep and tumbling creek on John Welthen's HOn3 layout was brushed on just as it began to cure. You can only work a few inches at a time, however.

Fig. 17-6 Frank Barone was able to tilt his entire 2 x 4-foot layout to pour these rapids on a new level. He then picked at the surface with a stick as it was curing to create the ripples.

Some plastics supply stores sell little beads of plastic about 1/32-inch in diameter that can be used to get the effect of rapids and other bubbling water. Experiment on your own to see if the beads produce the effect you want. They seem to work best with the use of almost-wet, not quite gelatin consistency resin. Some types of beads may be melted by the heat given off by the resin as it cures, but even that might produce the effect you want.

Be careful about using a spotlight or bare light bulb to form realistic ripples in the surface of the resin as it cures; that heat seems to promote some of those bubbles on the bottom. It's safer to dab the surface of the resin with an old spoon during that gelatin stage to form realistic surface ripples. You can use the same technique to carve wiggly "current" lines and waves in rivers or on the shores of harbors. One final note: be sure to take a good look at the resin from the normal viewing angle; if you can look over the edge of the table straight into it, a little extra blue or green dye might make it look even wetter and deeper. If you're looking at the "water" from almost a surface level, you may get the best effects with no dye whatsoever.

XVIII

Trees

One of the most surprising areas of techno-logical development in the hobby has been in the making of trees. The bottle-brush pine tree, baby's breath, asparagus fern and lichen forests were disturbed only by the ground foam and aluminum wool, and the check cancellation leaves for decades. Recently, though, some new products and new discoveries have made scale-model trees even more realistic. The photographs don't really do these trees justice because the photograph doesn't capture the texture effect that is there. People like John Olson and Paul Scoles have developed some real breakthroughs in pine tree technology, and kits for deciduous trees as well as some conifers from Woodland Scenics and AHM have broadened the modeler's choices of trees considerably. If there is such a thing as a single secret to scenery-making, it is to make as many different kinds of foliage textures as you can. These new ideas can certainly help do that. It's not enough to mix different sizes and shapes of trees or even to mix leaf trees with needle-bearing trees; the trunk and leaf or needle textures must also be as

varied as possible to capture that same effect in nature.

There are several brands of tree kits from Campbell, Architectural, Preiser, Kibri, AHM, Color-Rite and SS Limited, and I would recommend that you buy at least a half-dozen of every one of these, because each one will give you a slightly different texture. I'd also suggest that you supplement even that variety with some homemade trees to obtain the variegated texture effect that is so necessary for a realistic model scene. You can also combine the foliage materials and the tree trunks from any one of these commercial sources with those of any other to vary the shape and size of the trees. Add the variety you can obtain by combining some home-made leaf and needle textures and some homemade trunks, and you finally have something close to the kind of variety that Mother Nature offers in just about every model-railroad-size scene.

Balsa wood seems to make the best trunks for homemade pine trees. The material is easy to carve, and the bark texture can be done with a few swipes with a coarse wire brush or (for redwoods) a wire-bristle dog brush. The wood can be cut with a knife to produce very realistic splits and perpendicular cracks that are common to most types of pine trees. If you don't live near the area you are modeling, then find some back issues of *National Geographic* or perhaps the Time-Life Nature Series book *The Forests* to serve as a guide. You really do not know what a pine tree looks like until you study its shape and texture and color. The same lessons apply to creating trunks for deciduous trees from clothes-line cable or stranded steel picture-hanging wire and putty-type epoxy.

You will be able to get more trees for less money if you buy the 1" x 3" or ½" x 3" planks rather than square lengths. Use a hand saw or a jigsaw like Dremel's Moto-Shop to cut the balsa into wedges that taper from that 1 inch (or ½ inch) down to nothing in 12 to 18 inches of length (for most HO scale trees). You should be able to get at least a dozen 1-inch root area tree trunks and two dozen ½-inchers from a 3-inch by 3-foot plank of balsa.

Fig. 18-1   The only way to achieve realistic foliage is to vary the textures as much as Lonnie Shay (and of course Mother Nature) did on his HOn3 layout.

Fig. 18-2   Small clumps of cut hemp rope or the hairy inside of cattails are two alternative textures for this type of weed.

If you want a slightly wider stump end, graft on (with white glue) part of the tapered top from one of the other trunks, and use the broken one as one of the many struck-by-lightning topless trees that are seen in the forest. Hobby shops that carry model airplane supplies will have the balsa wood. Get some ⅛-inch doweling and cut it into 2-inch pieces. Drill the base of each tree trunk to fit the dowel, glue half the dowel's length into the tree, and insert the remaining half in a ⅛-inch hole in a board for the carving and tree-making process. When the tree is done, insert it into a ⅛-inch hole in the scenery.

When you're carving those trunks, remember to make a few of them with that split-by-lightning effect, and on some, add a trace or two of a giant piece of the root system carved from a scrap of balsa. Use some inexpensive artist's acrylic paints and water to get the correct trunk color, with some black for those burnouts.

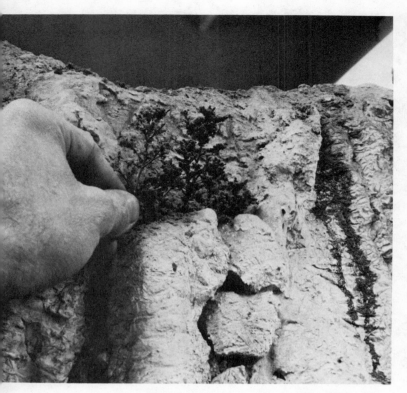

The branches are next, inserted into 1/32" or smaller holes drilled in the trunks. Florist shops sell the dried Caspia plants that Lonnie Shay uses. Try to get both the kind with small flowers on them and bare ones. Use the ones with flowers to simulate pine trees with long and bushy needle clusters and the naked Caspia branches (you may have to knock the flowers off yourself) for less-dense pines. Remember to include the dead branches that appear near the bottoms of most pine trees. Glue each branch into its hole by dipping it first into white glue. Move the branches around, and if necessary drill a few more holes until you get the effect you want. When you're satisfied, spray the branches lightly with a color like the trunk's shade.

The actual pine needles, even on the "flowered" Caspia branches, will be simulated with Woodland Scenic's, AHM's or Architectural's most finely ground foam rubber in a dark green or conifer shade. Experiment with the flat or matte-finish urethane sprays, like Varathane's FLAT clear urethane, to find one that will work for you. Spray the branches

Fig. 18-3 Real weeds, colored with latex paint, can be used to simulate small trees or bushes. Drill a small hole in the plaster; glue stem of the weed in place.

Fig. 18-4 The lichen on the left is the coarse root portion that most modelers throw away. Treated with glued-on ground foam, it looks even more realistic than the fine tips of lichen (right).

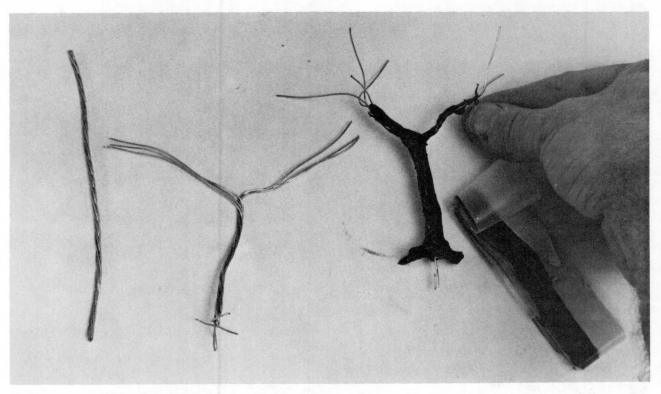

Fig. 18-5 The three stages in making tree trunks from clothesline cable (shown) or picture-hanging wire with stick-type epoxy putty for the bark of the trunk and major tree limbs.

Fig. 18-6 Three of the commercial ground-foam style tree kits (l to r): Architectural Models, Woodland Scenics and AHM See-Niks.

Fig. 18-7   Lonnie Shay uses carved balsa wood trunks for his pine trees, with Caspia plants dried and painted for the branches and Woodland Scenics foam for additional needle texture.

Fig. 18-8   A pin vise can be used to drill the holes for the Caspia branches.

with the urethane and dip them into a box of the ground foam. If you think it's necessary, spray the tree lightly with a flat-finish dark green to give the Caspia a bit more life—do keep the spray from the trunk, though, by aiming it at just the tips of the branches.

When you're ready to "plant" the trees, have some of whatever you use for "dirt" ready to cover the area where the tree trunk joins the plaster scenery. Real dirt, sifted through one of the fine-mesh plumber's screens or ladies' nylons, is the best. Place some of the bare (but painted light grey) Caspia branches around the area to simulate broken limbs. John Olson uses ground-up pine needles from the decomposed layer a few inches below the needles around the base of the tree for "pine needles" around the bases of his HO scale pines. Plant the pines in clumps of three or more with some variety in their sizes. Include a few "dead" pines made just like the "live" ones, but with grey-colored branches and trunks and no Caspia flowers or ground foam on the limbs. The process takes almost as long to describe as it does to do; you can probably make four or five trees in an hour. It will take fewer than you might think to give the effect of a dense forest.

These same tree-making techniques can be used to make other varieties of pine trees by substituting dried (and painted with green acrylic spray) asparagus fern or air fern, a living plant, for the Caspia branches. Florists can supply the asparagus or air fern. Include at least one or two trees of both types in a Caspia pine-tree forest just to give the look of endless variety that is so typical of nature. Plant a few lichen-and-ground-foam bushes in the vicinity of the pine tree trunks, and

Fig. 18-10 Lonnie Shay created a small lightning-caused burn area around the six trees to the left by blackening part of the trunks and removing the "flowers" from the Caspia stems.

Fig. 18-9 The pines in the foreground have asparagus fern branches. Those in the rear have Caspia plant and ground-foam branches.

have at least one "felled" tree and a jagged stump or two to complete the scene. Woodland Scenics makes some cast metal stumps that are perfect for this purpose, or carve them from balsa. Add a few cut tree stumps even if you're not modeling a logging railroad. If you are trying to create a logging line, use the balsa tree-carving techniques to make your logs, but cut the ends with an X-Acto razor saw to leave the splintered center that's common to most cut log ends.

Fig. 18-11 Gordon Johnson has combined many types of trees, including several made with carved trunks and air fern branches and "needles," to create this deep woods scene on his HO scale logging layout.

Sources of Supply

Your best source for any model railroad item is your nearest hobby dealer. Look in the telephone book's yellow pages under the heading "Hobby & Model Construction Supplies—Retail" for the names and addresses of the dealers nearest your home. If you cannot locate what you need at your local shop, then have your dealer write directly to the manufacturer to find out how he can obtain the product. If you want to obtain the catalogs or information from the manufacturers, enclose a stamped, self-addressed envelope for a reply or you probably won't get one. Most of them charge for their catalogs, so ask for a current price; some are as much as $5, others are just 25¢. Do try to buy everything you can from your local hobby dealer rather than shopping the discount stores for sales. The discounters won't have that piece of bass wood or that single casting, or the advice and help that a hobby dealer does. If you do have to pay "full list" for a locomotive, then consider it your rental fee on that inventory of smaller supplies your dealer keeps available for you. If you find it necessary to write di-

rectly to the manufacturers, here are my suggestions.

ADDM, Inc.
Route 1, Box 1802
Davis, CA 95616

AHM (Associated Hobby Manufacturers)
621 E. Cayuga Ave.
Philadelphia, PA 19120

A.I.M. Products
P.O. Box 5201
Greensboro, NC 27403

Alco Models
P.O. Box 211
Port Jefferson, NY 11777

Alexander Scale Models
P.O. Box 7121
Grand Rapids, MI 49510

Ambroid Products Co.
612 Montello St.
Brockton, MA 02403

Apag Hobbies, Inc.
Box 3521
Fullerton, CA 92634

Athearn
1510 W. 135th St.
Gardena, CA 90249

Atlas Tool Co.
378 Florence Ave.
Hillside, NJ 07205

B-K Enterprises
Rt. 2, Box 31
Barton, WI 54812

Bachmann Brothers, Inc.
1400 E. Erie Ave.
Philadelphia, PA 19124

Badger Air Brush Co.
9201 W. Gash
Franklin Park, IL 60131

Bowser Manufacturing Co.
21 Howard St.
Montoursville, PA 17754

Boyd Models
1835 Whittier Ave.
Costa Mesa, CA 92627

Caboose Industries
1861 Ridge Dr.
Freeport, IL 61032

CalScale
P.O. Box 475
Pinedale, CA 93650

Camino Scale Models
P.O. Box 666
Cottage Grove, OR 97424

Campbell Scale Models
P.O. Box 121
Tustin, CA 92680

Cary Locomotive Works
308 Three Oaks Rd.
Cary, IL 60013

Central Valley
13000 Saticoy St.
No. Hollywood, CA 91605

Champion Decal Co.
P.O. Box 1178
Minot, ND 58701

Color-Rite Scenery Products
2041 Winnetka Ave. N.
Minneapolis, MN 55427

ConCor (JMC International)
1025 Industrial Dr.
Bensenville, IL 60106

Craftsman Specialty Supply
6608 Forty Mile Point
Rogers City, MI 49779

Detail Associates
P.O. Box 197
Santa Maria, CA 93454

Details West
P.O. Box 5132
Hacienda Heights, CA 91745

Dremel Manufacturing Co.
4915 21st St.
Racine, WI 53406

Dyna-Model Products Co.
Sangerville, ME 04479

English
(*see Bowser*)

Faller (Chas. C. Merzbach Co.)
1107 Broadway
New York, NY 10010

Far East Distributors (F.E.D.)
Box 423
Seattle, WA 98111

Fine Scale Miniatures
49 Main St.
Peabody, MA 01960

Floquil-Polly S Color Corp.
Cobbleskill, NY 12043

GH Products
P.O. Box 3151
Irving, TX 75061

G R Signaling
28504-93 Sand Canyon Rd.
Canyon Country, CA 91351

General Tool
(*see Walthers*)

Golden West Books
P.O. Box 8136
San Marino, CA 91108

Grandt Line Products
2709 Los Aromas
Oakland, CA 94611

Newton K. Gregg Publisher
P.O. Box 868
Novato, CA 94947

HO West
20232 E. Damerel Dr.
Covina, CA 91722

Heath Co.
Benton Harbor, MI 49022

Herald King
(*see Miller Advertising*)

Highball Products
P.O. Box 43633
Cincinnati, OH 45243

Hobbytown of Boston
P.O. Box 82, Essex Station
Boston, MA 02112

Holgate & Reynolds
601 Davis St.
Evanston, IL 60201

Howell-North Books
  1050 Parker St.
  Berkeley, CA 94710

I.S.L.E. Laboratories
  (Mountains-in-Minutes)
  8302 Sylvania Metamora Rd.
  Sylvania, OH 43560

j-c Models
  Box 445
  South Bound Brook, NJ 08880

Kadee Quality Products Co.
  720 So. Grape St.
  Medford, OR 97501

Kalmbach Publishing Co.
  1027 No. Seventh St.
  Milwaukee, WI 53233

Kemtron Corp.
  P.O. Box 360
  Walnut CA 91789

Kibri (Models International)
  22524 Woodward Ave.
  Ferndale, MI 48220

LaBelle Industries (lubricants)
  1025 Industrial Dr.
  Bensenville, IL 60106

LaBelle Woodworking Co.
  P.O. Box 22
  Oconomowoc, WI 53066

Lambert Associates
  3353 Burdeck Dr.
  Oakland, CA 94602

Life-Like Products, Inc.
  1600 Union Ave.
  Baltimore, MD 21211

Lionel div. of General Mills Fun Group
  26750 23-Mile Rd.
  Mount Clemens, MI 48043

Little Depot
  1238A So. Beach Blvd.
  Anaheim, CA 92804

Loggers Supply
  69 Northridge Dr.
  St. Joseph, MO 64506

Mantua
  Woodbury Heights, NJ 08097

Mason Locomotive Works
  P.O. Box 4631
  Sylmar, CA 91342

Micro Scale (decals)
  1821 E. Newport Circle
  Santa Ana, CA 92705

Miller Advertising (Herald King)
  1627 Lilac Dr.
  Manitowoc, WI 54220

MDC (Model Die Casting, Inc.)
  P.O. Box 926
  Hawthorne, CA 90250

MRC (Model Rectifier Corp.)
  2500 Woodbridge Ave.
  Edison, NJ 08817

Model Power
  180 Smith St.
  Farmingdale, NY 11735

Mountains-in-Minutes
  (*see I.S.L.E. Industries*)

NJ Brass
  22 W. Nicholai St.
  Hicksville, NY 11801

Northeastern Scale Models
  P.O. Box 425
  Methuen, MA 01844

Northwest Short Line
  Box 423
  Seattle, WA 98111

PFM (Pacific Fast Mail)
  P.O. Box 57
  Edmonds, WA 98020

Paasche
  (*see Walthers*)

Penn Line
  (*see Bowser*)

Plastruct, Inc.
  1621 No. Indiana St.
  Los Angeles, CA 90063

Precision Scale Co.
Rt. 1, Box 1802
Davis, CA 95616

Preiser
(*see ConCor*)

Proto Power West
390 Santa Isabel
Costa Mesa, CA 92627

Quality Craft Models
177 Wheatley Ave.
Northumberland, PA 17857

Rail Craft
2201 Atwater St.
St. Louis, MO 63133

SS Limited
50 Freeport Blvd.
Sparks, NV 89431

Scotia Scale Models
(*see Walthers*)

Shay Wood Miter
(*see Walthers*)

Bob Sloan
30 E. Pleasant Rd.
St. Paul, MN 55110

Suncoast Models
P.O. Box 785
Black Mountain, NC 28711

Suydam & Co.
P.O. Box 55
Duarte, CA 91010

Thayer & Chandler
(*see Floquil*)

Timberline Models
P.O. Box 625
Golden, CO 80401

Train-Miniatures of Illinois
P.O. Box 292
S. Holland, IL 60473

Troller Corp.
3910 W. Montrose Ave.
Chicago, IL 61618

Tru-Scale Models
Johnson County Industrial Airport
RR 5
Olathe, KS 66061

Tyco Industries
Morristown, NJ 08057

Utah Pacific
P.O. Box 8174
Salt Lake City, UT 84108

Vollmer
(*see Boyd Models*)

Wm. K. Walthers, Inc.
5601 W. Florist Ave.
Milwaukee, WI 53218

Westwood
P.O. Box 2412, Station C
Fort Wayne, IN 46807

Whistle Stop Inc.
3745 E. Colorado Blvd.
Pasadena, CA 91107

Woodland Scenics
P.O. Box 266
Shawnee Mission, KS 66201

Publications

The Model Railroading Handbook
    Chilton Co.
    Radnor, PA 19089
        (Vol. I) $7.95 paperback, $15 hard-
        back

National Model Railroad Association
    P.O. Box 2186
    Indianapolis, IN 46206
        Annual membership $10 (includes
        monthly NMRA Bulletin)
        NMRA DATA-PAK $10

Railroad Model Craftsman magazine
    monthly
    P.O. Box 700
    Newton, NJ 07860
        $11 per year ($1 per issue)

Model Railroader magazine
    monthly
    1027 No. Seventh St.
    Milwaukee, WI 53233
        $14 per year ($1.25 per issue)

Great World of Model Railroading
    (biannually)

Argus Publishers
    12301 Wilshire Blvd.
    Los Angeles, CA 90025
        $2 per issue

Railroad Modeler magazine
    monthly
    Challenge Publications
    7950 Deering Ave.
    Canoga Park, CA 91304
        $18 per year ($2 per issue)

Narrow Gauge & Short Line Gazette
    bimonthly
    One First St., Suite C
    Los Altos, CA 94022
        $12.50 per year ($2.25 per issue)

Railfan
    bimonthly (prototype railroads)
    P.O. Box 700
    Newton, NJ 07860
        $6 per year ($1 per issue)

Trains
    monthly (prototype railroads)
    1027 No. Seventh St.
    Milwaukee, WI 53233
        $14 per year ($1.25 per issue)

Index

Page numbers in **bold** type indicate
information in illustrations